Salvador A

Revolutionary Lives

Series Editors: Brian Doherty, Keele University; Sarah Irving, University of Edinburgh; Professor Paul Le Blanc, La Roche College, Pittsburgh

Revolutionary Lives is a series of short, critical biographies of radical figures from throughout history. The books are sympathetic but not sycophantic, and the intention is to present a balanced and, where necessary, critical evaluation of the individual's place in their political field, putting their actions and achievements in context and exploring issues raised by their lives, such as the use or rejection of violence, nationalism, or gender in political activism. While individuals are the subject of the books, their personal lives are dealt with lightly except insofar as they mesh with political concerns. The focus is on the contribution these revolutionaries made to history, an examination of how far they achieved their aims in improving the lives of the oppressed and exploited, and how they can continue to be an inspiration for many today.

Published titles:

Leila Khaled: Icon of Palestinian Liberation
Sarah Irving

Jean Paul Marat: Tribune of the French Revolution
Clifford D. Conner

Sylvia Pankhurst
Suffragette, Socialist and Scourge of Empire
Katherine Connelly

Gerrard Winstanley: The Digger's Life and Legacy
John Gurney

www.revolutionarylives.co.uk

Salvador Allende

Revolutionary Democrat

Victor Figueroa Clark

PlutoPress
www.plutobooks.com

First published 2013 by Pluto Press
345 Archway Road, London N6 5AA

www.plutobooks.com

Distributed in the United States of America exclusively by
Palgrave Macmillan, a division of St. Martin's Press LLC,
175 Fifth Avenue, New York, NY 10010

British Library Cataloguing in Publication Data
A catalogue record for this book is available from the British Library

ISBN   978 0 7453 3308 3   Hardback
ISBN   978 0 7453 3307 6   Paperback
ISBN   978 1 8496 4933 9   PDF eBook
ISBN   978 1 8496 4934 6   Kindle eBook
ISBN   978 1 8496 4935 3   EPUB eBook

Library of Congress Cataloging in Publication Data applied for

This book is printed on paper suitable for recycling and made from fully managed
and sustained forest sources. Logging, pulping and manufacturing processes are
expected to conform to the environmental standards of the country of origin.

10   9   8   7   6   5   4   3   2

Typeset from disk by Stanford DTP Services, Northampton, England
Simultaneously printed digitally by CPI Antony Rowe, Chippenham, UK and
Edwards Bros in the United States of America

To Salvador and all the children of exile,
to my parents, and above all to Marcela.

There are men who struggle for a day, and they are good.
There are others who struggle for a year, and they are better.
There are some who struggle many years, and they are better still.

But there are those who struggle all their lives, and these are the
indispensible ones.

Bertolt Brecht

Contents

Acknowledgements

My thanks are due to the many people who helped me during the writing of this book, especially those family and friends who read early drafts of the manuscript and sent invaluable articles, interviews and other sources my way. Thanks also to David and Sarah at Pluto for their incisive comments, and to Carla and Boris at the Salvador Allende Foundation in Santiago for their help with the Foundation's excellent archive of speeches, books, documents and audiovisual materials. *Gracias* also to Marcelo Navarrete for his invaluable research.

Finally, my warm thanks to Jorge Arrate, a Minister in Allende's government, a brilliant presidential candidate, and the man who really made me think about the meaning of '*Allendismo*'.

More information relating to Allende's life and the history of Chile can be found on the Revolutionary Democrat facebook page (www.facebook.com/SalvadorAllendeRevolutionaryDemocrat). Intended to accompany the book, the page contains extra information, excerpts from interviews, music, photographs, interview footage and other clips that will enrich your understanding of Allende the man, and of the Chilean left as a social and political movement for change.

All photographs courtesy of the Salvador Allende Foundation.

1
Introduction

Most politicians are known for what they did in life rather than for the way they died. In this, as in so many things, Salvador Allende was an exception. More people know about his overthrow than know about what his government did, or how he became president of Chile. Allende's life, like that of so many other revolutionaries, has been stripped of context and reduced to the symbolism of his last moments when, surrounded by the smoke and flames of a bombed and burning presidential palace, he took his own life.

Allende's last words to the Chilean people were probably the greatest words of farewell ever uttered by a political leader, and they had an immense impact on people around the world. Yet there is much more to the life of Salvador Allende than the last seven hours, or even the last three years of his life. These were the culmination of his political ambitions, and the triumph of his political methods, but they were also the last stage in a long process of struggle and organisation that had its roots in the beginning of the twentieth century at around the time Allende was born. Allende's death and the overthrow of his government are often told as a dramatic tragedy, but Allende's significance for Chile and for the wider world also lies within the story of his life, intertwined in history of the popular movement that he led.

Chile's Popular Unity government was of tremendous interest during the early 1970s. The successful implementation of a 'peaceful road' happened to chime with the USSR's public recognition that a 'peaceful road' to socialism was possible, and it was of great interest to a Western European and North American left that shared its political methods if not always its revolutionary goals. The Chilean process was also of great interest to the Third World and the countries of the Non-Aligned

Key

...... National border

_ _ _ .' Provincial boundary (pre 1976)

▲ Major copper mine

⧅ Location of main nitrate fields

Index to provinces

1. Tarapaca	14. Ñuble
2. Antofagasta	15. Concepción
3. Atacama	16. Arauco
4. Coquímbo	17. Bio Bio
5. Aconcagua	18. Malleco
6. Valparaiso	19. Cautín
7. Santiago	20. Valdivia
8. Colchagua	21. Osorno
9. O'Higgins	22. Llanquihue
10. Curico	23. Chiloé
11. Talca	24. Aisén
12. Maule	25. Magallanes
13. Linares	

Map of Chile

Movement, who recognised in Allende's Chile a country that struggled with the same problems of exploitation and under-development. Allende's victory in September 1970 was therefore an event of global importance, which inadvertently and inevitably dragged Chile towards what one of Allende's erstwhile friends called 'the precipice of the Cold War.'[1]

Allende's victory was just as important to his ideological opponents. For the Chilean elite it marked the failure of constitutional means to hold back social pressure for fundamental changes. For Christian Democrats it highlighted the abject failure of their 'revolution in liberty', the effort to make deep social changes within capitalism, and while aligned with the United States. Further afield it was also the death knell of Washington's Alliance for Progress, a decade-old programme of economic and military measures designed to prevent revolution in the region and ostensibly promote 'development' through free trade and political liberalism. By the late 1960s it was clear that while it had successfully prevented revolution, often through dictatorship and repression, it had failed to achieve anything else. Chile, with its relatively well-developed political system and strongly rooted political parties, was therefore an important example of a civilian US-aligned government. Allende's election thus hit an exposed nerve. The United States had been actively involved in preventing a Marxist government in Chile since the early 1960s, spending millions of dollars and penetrating Chilean politics at every level. This made it even worse that Salvador Allende, a self-proclaimed Marxist, had been elected and that to top it all one of the main pillars of his government was the region's largest and best-organised Communist Party. The United States had helped overthrow Latin American governments for much less.

It was not just the failure of the Alliance for Progress and its efforts to subvert Chilean democracy that irked the United States. Allende's government had an economic and foreign policy programme that put it on a collision course with Washington. The nationalisation of copper and other natural resources created an example that could be emulated by many other Third World countries, and its foreign policy directly challenged US efforts to align Latin American countries behind Washington by claiming

Chile's inalienable right to determine its own foreign policy, free of US dictates – a complete rejection of the Monroe Doctrine that had justified US interventionism in Latin America since 1823. For the United States the appearance of a Marxist government was completely unacceptable. Détente between superpowers was one thing, allowing Chile to 'go communist', as Kissinger put it was another. The US government was not the only enemy of the Popular Unity. Other right-wing regimes, transnational corporations and individual businessmen from around the world were also opposed to it. In Brazil, where in 1964 the military had overthrown Joao Goulart, a president with similar aspirations to Allende, there was particular opposition. The Popular Unity was therefore at the centre of an ideological conflict that went beyond spheres of influence and economic interest and to the heart of a global struggle.

The Popular Unity government and its overthrow were thus a defining moment of Cold War politics. It frightened and inspired in equal measure. In Italy its overthrow led to the 'historic compromise' between Communists and Christian Democrats, in France to the construction of a Socialist-Communist coalition led by Francois Mitterand. Many people learned from studying the Popular Unity and its overthrow, and many more also heard about it first hand from the hundreds of thousands of Chileans the dictatorship forced into exile. Chile thus became a global revolutionary reference.

Allende's government has also been a reference point for today's progressive Latin American governments, with Venezuela the best-known example. These all won government through electoral means, and are to one degree or another implementing gradual transformations of society and economy. Although in a different period in history, they too are attempting to build forms of socialism. In this process, the spectre of Chile has loomed large and history has seemed to repeat itself – US funded opposition, bosses lock-outs, efforts to split trade unions and the popular movement, coups promoted in the military, media hysteria and political pressure in the international arena. Success in overcoming these challenges has owed much to lessons learned from Allende's overthrow.

Salvador Allende was a tireless champion of Latin American integration and self-determination, picking up the legacy of the liberators of Chile, and by extension, the legacy of Simon Bolivar. Allende helped establish the Andean Pact, and in a region full of dictatorships he sought to build foreign relations based on mutual respect and non-interference. The Popular Unity was therefore an ideological precursor to the integrationist efforts being made in the region today.

In Chile Allende's life and legacy were forbidden topics during the long dictatorship that followed his overthrow. Yet the two processes have created modern Chile. Pinochet's regime was the antithesis of Allende's, but it was unable to extinguish the memory of the Popular Unity, and it was unable to destroy what one of the Junta members called 'the cancer of Marxism'. Nor did it completely undo Allende's lifelong project to nationalise the copper industry, which remains the mainstay of the Chilean economy. Therefore the story of Allende's life, and the story of the popular movement that he helped to shape, are key to understanding what Chile is today.

Henry Kissinger once told a visiting Chilean foreign minister that, 'nothing important can come from the south. History has never been produced there.'[2] Yet Allende's political thought, and his efforts to build a revolutionary coalition remain relevant wherever there are people seeking to transform their societies away from capitalism. It was this potential that was one of the causes of Allende's overthrow. The 1970s was an ideologised period, and the language of Marxism was well known, hotly debated by left-wingers. In his own time Allende was called a 'reformist', and accused of 'parliamentarism'. Today, in a world without 'isms' we can see the revolutionary content of his thought more clearly, away from what Allende called 'the cold maze of theory'.[3] Throughout his life Allende pushed for a process of revolutionary reformism, to achieve a qualitative change in society. Although others misunderstood him, he never lost sight of this goal. Allende's life shows that political compromises do not have to be reformist, or aimed at preserving capitalism, and that in fact, reforms, by building upon and within existing structures, can become a revolutionary 'perestroika', avoiding the carnage and waste of violent change.

Allende came to lead a vast popular movement, which had three main motors, the country's two Marxist parties, and its unified trade union movement. As the century progressed Chile developed a rich network of social and political organisations and a profound political culture. Although positioned within the left, Allende was able to appeal to those beyond the popular movement, and this is why he became its pre-eminent figure. Throughout his life Allende sought to 'cultivate consciousness', and how Allende was able to do so is the story of the breadth of his political vision, the energy of his political methods, and the charisma of his personality.

In a measure of his importance to Chile, in 2008, 100 years after his birth, the Chilean public voted Allende the greatest Chilean in history. Forty years after his overthrow Allende remains a symbol of a Chile that was and yet could be. Even today Chileans remain divided by the twin legacy of the Popular Unity and the dictatorship that consumed it. Allende feared civil war because of the 'tremendous and painful' social and economic scars it would leave, while destroying the 'national community'. Yet despite his efforts Chile was subjected to a form of civil war from which it has yet to recover.

Because of this Allende has remained a figure of fascination in Chile, and throughout the Spanish-speaking world. Yet few biographies of Allende exist in English, and most of these were written shortly after his death in 1973. Naturally, the emphasis of these works was on the final years of his life and there was an inclination to make the books serve the purpose of solidarity with the victims of the coup. For this reason even the manner of his death was twisted, leading to long years of doubt over the manner of his end. Some aspects of his life, most notably regarding his character and personality were also ignored or overlooked. The many memoirs that have been published by friends and collaborators in the years since allow us today to fill out the picture of Allende's life as a politician and as a man. Now we can have a much richer, livelier, more human version of this extraordinary man who did so much to shape the destiny of his country, and by doing so has influenced Latin America and the World.

＊ ＊ ＊

Chile, the land of Salvador Allende's birth, is a long and narrow country that stretches 5,000 kilometres from the desert border with Peru down through a warm central region, onwards through a temperate southern zone where it begins to break up into islands and fjords. Far to the south, a short distance from Antarctica, it ends in the windswept and rainy plains of Tierra del Fuego. Isolated from the rest of Latin America by deserts and the mountainous spine formed by the high Andes, and facing the vastness of the Southern Pacific Ocean, Chileans have something of an island mentality. Chile's isolation and distance from world events have made Chileans somewhat self conscious in their provincialism, and very proud of those who have achieved international recognition.

Chile's original indigenous inhabitants, the Araucanian Mapuches, fiercely defended their independence for 300 years. Their courage and intelligence were admired by Spaniards such as the sixteenth century poet Alonso de Ercilla, who wrote that Chile produced people 'so remarkable, so proud, gallant and martial, that they have never by king been ruled nor to foreign dominion submitted.' Chile was a frontier country, and from war and trade the new 'mestizo' Chilean arose, a mixture of the Indigenous and Spanish peoples. After independence in 1818 new communities arrived from an industrialising and convulsed Europe, among them Allende's Belgian grandfather Arsene Gossens, although the majority of these immigrants were Germans. Yet despite this immigration, Chile's population remained remarkably homogenous, with only 4 per cent of the population being foreign-born in 1907.[4]

The vast majority of these people worked the land and toiled in the cities, or in mines and nitrate fields. Two contradictory stereotypes arose to describe the typical Chilean: the 'roto', and the 'huaso'. The 'roto' (literally 'the broken one'), the archetypal urban worker, tough, stubborn, cunning, opportunistic and uncouth. A dark-skinned *mestizo*, the *roto* was admired as a symbol of '*chilenidad*' (chileanness), the 'ethnic basis of the Chilean nation'.[5] Yet at the same time the *roto* was scorned for his poverty and ignorance, and for his lack of respect for the law, for his propensity to violence and rebellion, and for drunkenness. All ranks of society saw something of the '*roto*' in themselves, and so, as Loveman has described, the *roto* is 'a complex symbol of *chilenidad*, that signifies both the misery of the poverty-stricken worker and the '*viveza*' (opportunism) of those who benefit from his toil.'[6] The *huaso* was originally a poor rural worker and cowboy of a 'primitive roughness', within whom the 'screaming of the indian' subsisted.[7] Increasingly, rural landowners began to associate with this symbol of Chilean identity, completing it with flamboyant poncho, ornate wooden stirrups and silver spurs. These stereotypes developed through the nineteenth century, and were symbolic of Chile's increasing reliance on its growing mining industry and the agriculture of its central valley. This was the '*pueblo*', the people, who during the nineteenth century had begun to mobilise to improve their quality of life.

The Chile that Allende grew up in was the product of events that occurred during the late nineteenth century. Towards the end of this century Chile had come into conflict with its northern neighbour, Bolivia, over the allocation of income from nitrate mines that were located in Bolivian territory, but mostly manned and owned by Chileans. In 1879 the conflict escalated into war as Bolivia sought to impose taxes on foreign owned mines, including Chilean ones. Chilean troops moved north and rapidly conquered Bolivia's maritime provinces. Peru, which had a secret treaty with Bolivia, entered the war but was also defeated. By 1883 Chilean forces had occupied Lima. The result of the war was the annexation of Bolivia's maritime province, as well as some of southern Peru. Chile continued to occupy the Peruvian province of Tacna until 1925, when it was evacuated after the failure of a long-running and unpopular process of 'chileanisation'. The conflict left Chile in possession of the Atacama Desert, with its immense mineral riches, and a heightened sense of Chilean superiority over its neighbours, reinforcing ideas regarding the martial qualities of the 'Chilean race'. The Chilean army then turned south, and troops fresh from the deserts of the north completed the subjugation of the Mapuche indigenous people, opening up their lands for colonisation.

The War of the Pacific stimulated the industrialisation of Chile, thanks to the need to supply the army. After the war the workforce dedicated to nitrates and other forms of mining in the north expanded rapidly as both Chilean and foreign companies moved in. Chile experienced a population shift northwards, at the same time as this workforce became recognisably proletarian. Meanwhile the growth of industry and mining also stimulated changes within the elite. The new industrial elites sought greater political representation than Chile's aristocratic system allowed them. By the 1880s many of these wealthy mine owners had begun to question free trade, and were beginning to argue for forms of protectionism for Chile's nascent industry. The elite was also divided over religious issues, and the role of the Catholic Church in society. In 1886 José Manuel Balmaceda came to the Presidency, initiating the largest programme of public works yet seen with income from the nitrate mines. However, Balmaceda gradually alienated the landowning aristocracy, as well as a large number of Chilean nitrate impresarios, who feared his talk of the creation of a national nitrate company. This also threatened foreign nitrate barons, most notably, John Thomas North. North then began to use his fortune to undermine Balmaceda's government. Balmaceda did not seek mass political support, and his repression of Chile's first general strike in 1890 lost him much of what he had. Personality conflicts and problems dispensing patronage among his Liberal followers then ensured Balmaceda's increasing isolation.[8] In 1891 Congress declared his government unconstitutional and the navy rebelled, a short and bloody civil war followed, and Balmaceda's forces were defeated.

Following 1891, Chile was governed by a 'parliamentary republic' where most power lay with parliament, where 'elite interest groups dressed up as political parties vied for power and state patronage.'[9] Although restrictive in many ways, the parliamentary republic, founded by the revolution against Balmaceda's 'tyranny', did allow the development of free speech and some level of political opposition. The state role in the economy was reduced and foreign investment in nitrates increased. Thanks to income from nitrates taxes were gradually withdrawn. The income from mining and nitrates continued to stimulate development, and urbanisation increased, as did the role of mining in the economy. By 1907 44 per cent of the population was urban. Chilean society was overwhelmingly poor, uneducated, had no political representation and lived in extreme insecurity. By 1913 more than half of deaths recorded in Chile were infants under 5 years of age.[10] The social question became increasingly important, yet the parliamentary governments of the elite did not develop any social policies.

Meanwhile workers organisation expanded. Ever since independence some people had sought to make true its lofty ideals. By the middle of the nineteenth century this combined with the radicalising effects of the 1848 revolutions in Europe to lead to the first recognisably modern 'left-wing' organisations, such as The Society for Equality founded at the end of 1850.[11] Then in 1887 the Partido Democrata (Democratic Party) was founded to seek 'political, economic and social liberation of the people'.[12] As a response to poverty and injustice and under the influence of socialist and anarchist ideas, during the same period worker organisation and unrest grew. Workers' cooperatives, fraternities and incipient trade unions were founded and by the turn of the century strikes were commonplace. Lacking any social policies, the establishment responded with massacres of workers in Valparaiso in 1903, dockworkers in Antofagasta in 1906 and nitrate workers in the infamous massacre at Iquique in 1907. Repression was unable to prevent further popular mobilisation, and in 1907 workers founded the FOCH (Federation of Chilean Workers). Then, in 1912, workers disillusioned with the Democratic Party founded the Partido Obrero Socialista (Socialist Workers' Party), led by Luis Emilio Recabarren, a printworker originally from Valparaiso.

By the early twentieth century discontent with the way things were was not confined to the popular classes. Thirty years of studies, reports and investigations into the dire poverty of the masses had led many to seek some form of reform. Such obvious injustice cried out for change. The middle class was also unhappy at their exclusion from politics and at the routine injustices of Chilean society. Abroad, the Mexican and Russian revolutions showed radical change was possible. Thousands of people, including some of Chile's greatest figures, such as its Nobel prize-winning poets Pablo Neruda and Gabriela Mistral, shared this discontent and helped create new political movements. These men and women were products of a country undergoing immense socio-economic transformations at the beginning of the twentieth century and buffeted by the winds of change blowing across the world.

Most of Allende's peers looked to Europe, and prized rationalism, a solid education and high culture. They had benefited from the evolution of the Chilean state and from Chile's uneven and unjust economic development. In particular they were products of a well-developed education system, albeit one out of sync with a conservative political system. This generation could still hear the dim echoes of the ideals of independence. Born during the death throes of the old oligarchic society, Allende was shaped by an age where new social classes fought for their share of the nation's wealth and for a say in how society was run. It was a period in which people were moved by great ideals, where revolution was not a utopic dream but an evident possibility. Like many people across the world, Allende's thinking was shaped by the great ideology of the age: Marxism. It came to offer him a means of interpreting history, but also a way to end the alienation suffered by the vast majority of people. By freeing the people from exploitation, socialism also offered a way to liberate the oppressors, thus making real the ideals expressed in the American and French Revolutions. Allende lived his life in the cause of these ideas, and if he sought power it was to bring about the changes that would make such a country, and such a world, possible. By doing so he changed Chile and made an indelible mark on its people and its history.

2

Early Life and Youth

Salvador Allende Gossens was born on 26 June 1908 in the port city of Valparaiso.[1] He was the fourth child of Salvador Allende Castro and Laura Gossens Uribe, although the two babies that preceded him died in infancy. As was then the tradition in Chile, Allende was named after his deceased elder sibling, Salvador. His sister, Laura, born three years later, was similarly named after her elder sister. His was an established middle class professional family of distinguished radical lineage. On his father's side Allende was descended from a long line of revolutionary masons, men imbued with the ideals of the Latin American independence struggles, and the French and American revolutions and with an interest in secular education and modernisation.[2] His great-grandfather José Gregorio Allende Garcés was one of three Allende Garcés brothers famed for their valour who had fought alongside Chile's independence hero Bernardo O'Higgins. When O'Higgins was forced into exile, José Gregorio followed him there, fighting alongside Jóse de San Martín (the liberator of Argentina, Chile and Peru) and Simon Bolivar. His two brothers, Salvador Allende's great uncles, remained in Chile fighting the Spanish alongside the legendary guerrilla leader Manuel Rodríguez.

José Gregorio's son, Ramon Allende Padin, Salvador Allende's grandfather, became a renowned doctor, freemason, and Radical politician at a time when the Radical Party was the leading force for social change. As a doctor he was renowned for his charity and for providing medical assistance to the poor. He was elected to Congress in 1876, campaigning vigorously for the separation of church and state at a time when the Catholic Church dominated Chilean politics. He gave up the safety of his office to create the Chilean army's medical services in the 1879–83 war with Peru.

This war changed the socio-economic balance in Chile, and led to the strengthening of Chilean Liberalism. After the war Ramon Allende founded Chile's first secular school and became the dean of the Medical School of the University of Chile, as well as being re-elected to the Senate. Shortly before his death he was elected Grand Master of the Chilean freemasons. His renown was such that his funeral was attended by all the leading political figures of the day, and among his coffin bearers were two future presidents of Chile – José Manuel Balmaceda, and Ramon Barros Luco. Ramon Allende's political views and his red hair led to him being nicknamed 'Red Allende', which his grandson took great pride in.[3]

Although not as distinguished as Ramon Allende Padin, Ramon's son Don Salvador Allende Castro was also a man of radical political views, a lawyer and a freemason. Reputedly a charismatic man, with a talent for rhyming and mischievous poetry, Salvador Allende Castro was a former soldier who had fought for the Liberal President José Manuel Balmaceda in the brutal 1891 civil war that cost 30,000 lives. Balmaceda was overthrown in a naval rebellion supported and partly financed by British nitrate magnates who opposed his measures to tax the trade in order to finance the industrialisation and modernisation of Chile.[4] Balmaceda promoted the colonisation of the south of the country, and invested heavily in infrastructure upsetting the Chilean landowning and conservative elite by promoting universal suffrage and secular education, and by reforming the political system. Under Balmaceda the organisations of the working class began to develop, and the Democratic Party, the forerunner of the political parties of the Chilean left was founded.[5] Refuged in the Argentinean embassy the day after his elected mandate ran out and in the face of defeat, Balmaceda shot himself. In the post-war amnesty Salvador Allende Castro became a lawyer whose career took off when he was appointed appeals court lawyer in the Peruvian city of Tacna, then occupied by Chile, where the family lived for several years. However, Allende Castro was famed for his spendthrift ways and with his wages often arriving late the family was often heavily in debt.

On his mother's side Salvador Allende was descended from Arséne Gossens, a devout Catholic Belgian immigrant to Chile, who arrived in about 1860 and who later married Laura Uribe. Allende's mother, Laura Gossens Uribe, was brought up a religious woman, and the family's Catholic piety led them to take the other side in the 1891 civil war. Salvador Allende's uncle, Arsenio Gossens Uribe, was executed by Balmaceda's troops in August 1891. Allende's family had thus experienced the divisions and the brutality of civil war in his own family, and this was one of the reasons he later opposed a violent road to revolution.

Allende spent his early childhood in Tacna, in what is today Peru. It was here he received the nickname that family and old friends had for him – 'Chicho' – a mispronunciation of the diminutive of his name (*Salvadorchicho* instead of *Salvadorcito*). Tacna remained under Chilean occupation from 1880–1929, and Salvador spent several years in the city in close proximity to the Chilean army. It was here that he first learned to ride and to shoot. In Tacna Allende attended a mixed school for Chileans and Peruvians and picked up a love of spicy Peruvian cooking while making his first friendships. The children grew up in a tense atmosphere of increasingly active Peruvian resistance to efforts to 'Chileanise' the city. Inspired by a teacher's accounts of the independence of the principality of Monaco, some of the children proposed making Tacna independent. It was Allende's first idealist foray into politics.[6] In Tacna, the scene of intense political debate, the young Allende would regale his family with presidential speeches, one foot atop a small stool. It is possible that Allende was later uncomfortable with his family's role in the administration of occupied Peru, since he rarely spoke of this period. When the young Salvador was ten (1918), the Allende family moved south to Iquique, the capital of the nitrate exporting industry, and the scene of the infamous 1907 massacre of nitrate miners. Miners protesting slave-like working conditions demonstrated in the city, attracting more and more followers. Foreign mine-owners and their diplomatic representatives were concerned as to whether the state would be able to 'control' the situation and eventually up to 3,000 workers were gunned down by Chilean troops. Among the victims were women and children. Despite the killings, the city retained a reputation for political radicalism and Iquique was the scene of continual demonstrations. In 1919 the city was even put under martial law. Although Allende was only ten at the time, a close friend later wrote that Allende had witnessed workers' demonstrations and heard their slogans.[7] The brutal repression of workers' demands helped to undermine the legitimacy of the regime installed after 1891.

In 1919 the Allende family moved once more, this time to the Southern port city of Valdivia, on the old colonial border between the Mapuche nation and the Spanish colony and the scene of heavy German colonisation following the brutal Chilean conquest of the region in the 1880s. Allende attended a school where he was notable for his comparative worldliness and for having a waterproof coat. In 1921 the family returned to Valparaiso, where Allende finished school in 1924. The Chilean education system, funded by the taxation of the British-owned nitrate mines remained largely secular, and progressive. It enjoyed some independence from government. It was a system that tried to imbue students with modern ideas, and a healthy interest in physical education. Allende thrived at school, becoming national swimming and decathlon champion, and thanks to his prodigious memory and the help of discussions with friends, he achieved high grades without having to dedicate long hours to study.

Tacna, Iquique and Valdivia were all somewhat peripheral cities, but Valparaiso was one of the most important ports on the Pacific Ocean until it began a slow decline after the Panama Canal was completed in 1914. It had some 200,000 inhabitants and was a key stopping point for any ship travelling around Cape Horn. It attracted many immigrants, from the British expats who dominated the nitrate industry and set up the city's first cricket and football clubs to Italian anarchists such as Juan Demarchi, the shoemaker who Allende recalled lending him his first socialist literature and teaching him to play chess after school. In 1906 a terrible earthquake hit Valparaiso and much of its elite left the exposed slopes of the city for the safer and gentler hills of nearby Viña del Mar. By 1921 'Valpo' had a marked proletarian feel and a well-developed popular movement. The young Allende's life rotated around these two very different cities. In Valparaiso he socialised with the children of the middle and working classes, whereas in Viña del Mar he mixed with the offspring of the rich. In Valparaiso he played football and swam in the sea, in Viña del Mar he practised marksmanship and riding. In Valparaiso he learned at the footstool of an anarchist cobbler, in Viña del Mar Allende listened to Arturo Alessandri, the future president of Chile, discuss politics with his father, an old university friend. Salvador's elder sister married into the well-respected Grove family, who would also play an important role in Chilean politics, and who influenced the thinking of the young Salvador Allende. The combination of a distinguished family history and an elite upbringing gave the young Salvador a strong sense of his own worth, and a clearly defined set of behaviours expected of a 'man' of his station. At the same time his unsettled childhood must have forced him to establish friendships and his social status in each new place, which alongside a natural temper, contributed to the development of a sociable and yet combative personality.

Despite this easy access to wealth and power, his contact with the harsh realities of life in Valparaiso and an increasingly turbulent political atmosphere led him to later identify with the proud proletarian port city and not the gentle avenues of Viña del Mar, and in a 1972 interview with Regis Debray he called himself a proud '*porteño*' (the name for people from the port of Valparaiso) and Chile's first '*porteño*' president.

Salvador Allende finished school with excellent grades a year early at the age of 16. On the day he received his exam results Allende's classmates were discussing their future options. When they asked Salvador what he wanted to become he said 'I'm going to be president of Chile.'[8] Allende did not recall his classmates' reactions, but his answer underlined his early interest in politics, his ambition and a self-confidence bordering on arrogance. However, this arrogance was offset with a lively self-deprecating humour and a love of practical jokes. Allende had to decide between becoming a lawyer like his father or a doctor like his grandfather. Torn between the two Allende chose medicine because like his grandfather he wanted to 'serve the most poor and needy'.[9] It was not an easy decision however, and in later life he sometimes expressed regret at not following the law alongside his medical studies. On top of having to decide his professional future, Allende was affected by a confusing political situation that led to a period of 'perplexity and negativism'.[10] A corrupt congress dominated by factions of the elite ruled the country, and a few families controlled much of the nation's wealth, and yet the majority of Chileans lived lives of brutal poverty and harsh exploitation – often at the hands of foreign bosses. At the same time a new middle class was bursting onto the scene and it thirsted for representation. It was a time of feverish political debate, inspired by the Mexican and Russian revolutions. Workers and students in particular were actively visualising a better future. What role could a young man from the edges of the elite play in this future? The FECH students' federation newspaper 'Claridad' (Clarity) succinctly expressed the challenge facing the well-to-do youth of Chile in December 1920:

> You are a coward. Yes a complete coward. And don't think that we are saying this to attract you to this poster. No. Quite simply, you, whoever you are that is reading this, have you noticed how you live? What is it that you do every day? You are silent when convenient. You always ingratiate yourself with the more powerful. You opine like everyone else. When have you ever raised your voice against the scandalous infamy around you? When? Look back at your life. Tomorrow or maybe the day after you may die and what purpose have you served? Do you know what the society we live in is, this capitalist society? Do you know what the society is that we push for and that you try to delay? No doubt you think the same as 'El Mercurio', 'La Nacion', 'El Diario Ilustrado'[11] etcetera, the same as the newspaper you read everyday. Learn for yourself man. Don't be a puppet. Have some shame. Use your own head, that's what it's there for. Find out. Investigate. Don't be fearful. And don't leave calmly after reading this. In vain you try to be deaf. You are a coward, at the mercy of he who pays you best, or shouts at you loudest. Don't fool yourself. When have you ever said anything that could jeopardise you? Because of docile individuals like you the world is unliveable with swine.[12]

For Allende, the transition between a youthful interest in politics and political activism had only just begun. Across the world humanity seemed on the verge of something new, and yet Chile remained stuck in the past. Demands for change were greeted with repression, as in the notorious 1918 Jaramillo Law that allowed the expulsion of 'foreign subversives' and legalised armed repression of demonstrations. Despite this the pressure for change kept building.

Unlike many of his contemporaries, the young Allende had been exposed to the social inequality of Chilean society, and he knew the conditions people lived in far beyond the bay of Valparaiso. He had begun to question the status quo, but he needed time to think. As a remedy to his 'negativism' Allende prescribed himself a period in the ranks, postponing his entry into the university of Chile's medical school by a year. It was unheard of for a young man of his class to do this. Many even measured their social status by how easily they avoided their nominally compulsory service, but even as a young man Allende was an independent thinker. He duly joined the '*Coraceros*' cavalry regiment of the Chilean army, based in Viña del Mar where he polished the riding skills that came in very useful during his many electoral campaigns in remote areas, and improved his marksmanship. He ended his military service with a few weeks in Tacna, the Peruvian city still occupied by Chile.

His military experience was to mark Allende for life, and unlike many on the left, he was always comfortable with the military world. However, it did not sit well with his radical university friends who saw his service as a 'demonstration of ideological weakness'.[13] Others also wondered if he had joined in order to benefit from the romantic benefits of the uniform.[14] In fact it was in Tacna that Allende first gained a reputation as a womaniser. In the male society of the time this success brought Allende admiration and sometimes envy. To an extent it was expected of a successful man of his class, and character – a kind of confirmation of an exalted social status. No doubt Allende was influenced by his father – also a notorious womaniser. Allende tried to respond by arguing that the military had given him the opportunity to mix with men from other social classes, and therefore to learn more about Chile's social reality at first hand. It is also likely that Allende wanted to follow in the footsteps of his family tradition in the military. At this stage of his life Allende appears to have had a somewhat ambiguous attitude to the Chilean state, rebelling against its injustices, but as yet without a revolutionary mission. His experiences in the army, where he was punished for articulating 'collective complaints', helped to convince him that the military was no place for someone with social concerns, and Allende definitively turned towards medicine.[15]

Chile in the 1920s was a country in economic and social turmoil. The old oligarchic regime was weakening, and the state was incapable of answering social demands stimulated by the Mexican and Russian revolutions without making profound political and economic changes. Meanwhile the economy suffered from the collapse of Chile's nitrate export markets after the end of the First World War. Both workers and students were at the forefront of challenging the regime. In 1906 students had founded the FECH (Federation of Students of Chile), which became an increasingly radical critic of the establishment and the status quo. In 1912 Luis Emilio Recabarren and others split from the Democratic Party and formed the Partido Obrero Socialista (POS; Socialist Workers' Party), building on the vast growth in working class organisations that occurred after 1890. In 1922 the POS became the Communist Party of Chile. At the same time feminist groups were established across the country, many of them overlapping with workers' organisations. The elites unleashed a harsh anti-socialist campaign from the pulpit and from the pages of the elite-owned press, but neither these nor brutal repression were able to stifle the growth of socialist consciousness among the workers. In 1919 the FOCH (Federation of Chilean Workers) trade union federation declared the need to destroy capitalism. Anarchist trade unions were also set up under the IWW (International Workers of the World) in the same year. Mass demonstrations became increasingly common. Inflation was making food expensive and people began to starve. Fearful of revolution, some sectors within the elite supported putting forward a candidate who they hoped would be able to modernise the country while maintaining their social position.

Liberal, Democratic and Radical groups thus allied behind the incendiary rhetoric of the Allende's old family friend, Arturo Alessandri, the so-called 'Lion of Tarapaca' who provided an attractive populist alternative for the middle classes. He also gathered working class support with talk of his 'beloved rabble' while spitting fire at the 'golden swine' who ruled the country. Alessandri was elected president in mid 1920, despite the opposition of the most conservative elite who feared this 'Chilean Lenin' would end their predominance.[16] Despite Alessandri's victory, no single political force dominated the scene. Alessandri had attracted the middle classes, but they lacked an effective political vehicle for their aspirations, and the elite maintained its control of the political institutions and the levers of economic power. They resisted Alessandri's efforts to build a social security net, recognise trade unions and provide a labour code, blocking his reforms in the Senate. When the masses tried to claim the promises that they had been made, Alessandri responded with repression. The stalemate provoked the collapse of his government and its replacement by a progressive military junta on 11 September 1924. In January 1925 this Junta also fell, and Alessandri was recalled. With military support Alessandri proclaimed a new constitution in September 1925, but the structural issues remained the same. In such an unstable situation the political space for a strongman who could preserve the system began to emerge. One military officer began to establish himself as the power in the shadows, and by May 1927 Colonel Carlos Ibañez was able to have himself elected with 97 per cent support, calling for 'caution both above and below.'[17] The Ibañez dictatorship, which was to mark Allende's early political life, had begun.

The Allende that finished his military service in November 1925 had already developed many of the traits that came to define his personality. He was a fashionable young man, an accomplished athlete, a practical joker, a womaniser and a leader among his peers. In early 1926 he moved to Santiago to study medicine at the University of Chile, initially staying with an aunt. At university he studied hard, and took up boxing and Greco-Roman wrestling, as well as continuing to play chess. Allende even requested to sit exams for a law degree, but was turned down. A few months into his university life, Chile fell under the dictatorship of Carlos Ibañez del Campo, whose policies included opening up the country to US investment – notably in the copper mining industry – as well as the repression of the Communist Party and other workers' organisations. Drawing upon Italian fascist inspiration, Ibañez set up 'Peoples' Houses' where workers could relax in a suitably anti-communist atmosphere, as well as an Italian-modelled police force known as the '*Carabineros*'. Ibañez also began to borrow large amounts from foreign banks in order to fund public works. The brutality of the Ibañez dictatorship, its closure of the FECH students' union and its incapacity to resolve any of Chile's growing social and economic problems stimulated student opposition, although the bulk of the opposition to the dictatorship came from the organisations of the impoverished and repressed working class.

As soon as Allende could, he left his aunt's comfortable home and moved to the area near the Vega Central food market in Recoleta, one of Santiago's poorer neighbourhoods, where the majority of medical students lived. The environment encouraged political activism since the students lived with poverty all around them, and in the hospitals they encountered its effects. Soon afterwards Salvador's father became ill with diabetes and unable to provide for all his children while they studied. Salvador was therefore forced to find work, becoming an assistant in the hospital morgue, as well as working in a psychiatric hospital and teaching at a night school. This everyday contact with the toll of misery and poverty became his second university and played an important part in converting Allende's political concerns into revolutionary ideas.[18]

It was while he was a student that Allende began his political life. In his second year at university he was elected the President of the medical students' association (1927), historically one of the most combative of the University of Chile. Allende also joined a new organisation dedicated to democratising the university and achieving social justice. The 'Avance' group of students and intellectuals was one of several organisations promoted by the illegal Communist Party to reach out to society. It was made up of radicalised students united in their opposition to Ibañez and by their concerns for a university with the freedom to determine its own curricula, and develop a strong social commitment. It was in Avance that Allende began to study and analyse political texts. Allende recalled members gathering at night for 'readings of Das Kapital and Lenin, and also Trotsky.'[19] Allende impressed his comrades with his capacity to remember verbatim quotes from these texts having just heard them read. Through this work Allende was introduced to Marxist writings, but seems that at this stage Avance's leaders mostly valued Allende for his ability to garner female votes for Avance.[20]

In August 1930 the students re-established the FECH in defiance of Ibañez. Fiery discussions on what actions to take against the dictatorship were held in packed meeting halls. The still-small Avance group had its speakers booed off stage. In a somewhat desperate move Avance leaders put Allende forward to speak, because he looked like a 'toff', and was relatively unknown.[21] Hundreds of students filled the hall, whistling and shouting. Allende put his left hand in his jacket pocket, raised his right hand and began: 'Gentlemen!' A stunned silence followed.[22] This revolutionary had committed the heresy of not calling his fellows 'comrades'. Allende then spoke, avoiding the revolutionary slogans beloved of his friends, turning the debate into one on freedom of speech and political liberty. The speech marked his transformation into an important student leader, and soon afterwards Allende was elected vice president of the FECH. Allende then became a regular presence at demonstrations against the dictatorship and known to the police.

As the Great Depression hit Chile and the Ibañez dictatorship continued, the social situation reached revolutionary proportions. Over 200,000 workers from a population of some 4 million were thrown into unemployment. As a known student leader Allende was arrested and briefly imprisoned along with others accused of rabble rousing. Despite this Allende was also elected to the council of the University of Chile. From April to July 1931 the students were at the forefront of social mobilisations against the dictatorship. In July Ibañez was forced to assemble a civilian government of 'national salvation'. On 18 July the minister of the economy admitted the government was broke.[23] Meanwhile, mobilised by the Avance group, the students, Allende among them, seized the buildings of the University of Chile, declaring a national strike to bring down the dictatorship. Ibañez's Carabineros tried to dislodge them, but armed with pistols provided by their wealthy families they fought to defend positions on the rooftops of the university and upon the castellated walls of the Santa Lucia hill in central Santiago. Workers' demonstrations also brought together tens of thousands of people. Cavalry charges with lances and running battles took place across the centre of the city, hundreds of people were arrested, and over 20 were killed.[24] Funerals on 25 and 26 July drew over 100,000 people despite the repression. The unrest and the strikes made the country ungovernable. On 26 July Ibañez stepped down and was forced to flee the country. The crowds turned on the Carabineros and many were lynched.

The Ibañez dictatorship was replaced by the government of Juan Esteban Montero, Ibañez's former interior minister. To cope with the economic crisis this government attempted to cut public spending. One measure was to slash the pay of naval ratings by 30 per cent, affecting some 14,000 sailors and their families. The cuts led to a mutiny in August 1931 by sailors in Valparaiso, Coquímbo and Talcahuano. Officers were arrested and revolutionary committees established. In Valparaiso the Maipo regiment of the army went over to the mutineers. The sailors had broad social demands and they called for an agrarian reform, an end to foreign monopolies and the democratisation of the armed forces. The Chilean elite went into a frenzy. The press called it a 'Bolshevik uprising', a state of siege was declared and ultra-right wing groups set up a 'Citizen Guard'. However, the sailors were acting in the absence of a strong social movement. The unity of the struggle against the Ibañez regime had evaporated, and the revolutionary groups were weakened. Communists argued for 'Soviet power' – the creation of soviets of 'workers, peasants, soldiers and students', but few outside the left understood what this meant. A general strike failed to generate enough support. The student movement was also disabled by sectarian arguments. Allende, a participant in these discussions was expelled from 'Avance' when he argued against the copying of foreign experiences, and the exclusion of the professionals that the students would later become. As he later recalled, 'I said it was crazy [...] that I, as a student, didn't want to sign something that tomorrow, as a professional I couldn't accept.'[25] It was a harsh blow and it helped instil in him a lifelong dislike of dogmatism and sectarianism. As if that were not enough, Allende was also thrown out of university and was not readmitted until early in 1932.

The sailors' mutiny was put down by loyal army units and bombarded by the air force. Some 2,500 soldiers and sailors were killed in the fighting.[26] Ten of their leaders were sentenced to death, others to hard labour and some to internal exile on Easter Island or the cold islands of the far south. It was a revolutionary moment in a revolutionary time, but the left was too disorganised, too disunited and incapable of taking advantage of the chaos to unite with the sailors and take power. The government reversed the wage cut and began a severe repression of trade unions and left-wing organisations. In October 1931 Montero won new elections, but, like the captain of an immense sea vessel, he was unable to change the country's course because the economic system remained unchanged. The chaotic political situation and the repression of the left continued: on Christmas Day, 29 communists were hunted down and killed. In January 1932 workers called a general strike, which lasted two days before the armed forces and police put it down. Nor were the indigenous peoples of the south excluded from the ferment. In early 1932 the Mapuche declared an 'indigenous republic', identifying the indigenous struggle with that of the proletariat and calling for an alliance of indigenous peoples, peasants and workers. Its leaders were arrested and imprisoned.[27]

Meanwhile Salvador Allende returned to Valparaiso in order to complete his dissertation and to be near his ailing father. The political situation remained unstable, but some people exiled by Ibañez were able to return to Chile, among them Marmaduke Grove. A charismatic and mercurial man, Grove had been a key figure in conspiracies against Ibañez. He had been exiled first to Europe and then to Easter Island after supporting the mutinying sailors. In an effort to assuage his supporters in the military, upon his return to the mainland he was appointed commander of the Chilean air force. From this position he continued his plotting. The Montero government was incapable of resolving the deep structural crisis, or changing Chile's subordination to external interests that was in large part to blame for the economic situation, and the opposition grew. Finally, in June 1932, Marmaduke Grove led a military coup that overthrew the Montero government and declared a socialist republic in order to give 'bread, roof and clothing' to the people.

The revolutionary government's 40-point programme included controls on food distribution, the handover of uncultivated lands to peasants, the creation of state enterprises in key sectors, the nationalisation of banks, an amnesty of political prisoners, the creation of a cooperative sector of the economy, the opening of diplomatic relations with the Soviet Union and an end to foreign interference in Chilean affairs. One of the new government's most popular measures was to return property, often work tools that had been confiscated from poor debtors. The socialist republic terrified the Chilean elite and shocked the United States and the United Kingdom, both of which refused to recognise the revolutionary government. The United States also announced it was sending a naval squadron to the Chilean coast in order to 'protect private property'.[28] In Chile many on the left did not quite know how to place the new government, which called itself socialist but rejected communism. The Communist Party meanwhile rejected alliances with 'bourgeois' organisations – including the new socialist government. Instead it demanded that the government arm the people and create soviets of workers, soldiers and peasants. Some socialists in the government also called for the creation of a 'Popular Militia', but Grove refused to do this fearing the reaction of the armed forces. The socialist republic therefore lacked the support of a unified mass movement.

The revolutionary government was also divided with Carlos Davila, Ibañez's former ambassador to the United States, opposing many radical measures. Davila then led the military counter-revolution that deposed the socialist republic, although it claimed to be a continuation of the socialist government. Marmaduke Grove was exiled once more to Easter Island from where he would return to fight in the upcoming elections. In Valparaiso Salvador Allende defended the socialist republic at a public meeting in the Law Faculty of the University. His friendship with the Grove family was well known and, following the speech, Allende was arrested and imprisoned alongside Alfredo, his elder brother and Marmaduke's brother Eduardo. After being released by one military tribunal the two Allende brothers were re-arrested by another and court-martialled. While in prison their father became seriously ill, and the brothers were allowed to visit him on his deathbed. Their father had had one leg amputated, and gangrene was affecting the other. Salvador could see his father was dying. Since Don Salvador had no material wealth he told his sons that all he could leave them was a clean, honest upbringing. He died the next day. At his funeral, in a romantic gesture echoing Bolivar's liberation oath in Rome, Allende solemnly vowed to dedicate his life to the social struggle.

3

Reaching Political Maturity

In taking a vow at his father's graveside to dedicate his life to the social struggle, Allende took a step further than Ramon Padin, his illustrious grandfather. Ramon Allende had been a liberal, a philanthropist and a social reformer, but not a socialist. His grandson, imbued with a Marxist critique of capitalism, and influenced by the revolutionary times he was living, took the decision to struggle for a total transformation of society, building upon and extending the ideas of his progressive ancestors. In a society where in 1930 the average lifespan was 35.4 years for a man and 37.7 years for a woman, many of his contemporaries did likewise.[1] At the same time the organisations of the left had learned valuable lessons from the unrest of the late 1920s and early 1930s. The socialist republic had failed because it had not had organised mass support, because the left was divided, and because too many people had thought that it was enough to hold executive power, that socialism could be built by decree. In the Communist Party a fierce critique of the Party's role in the failure of the Republic led to a return to policies first used under the leadership of Luis Emilio Recabarren, policies of mass politics and alliance building. The failure of the Republic also led directly to the merger of the many smaller socialist groups and the founding of the Socialist Party of Chile on 19 April 1933.

Although Salvador Allende was not present at the Socialist Party's foundational congress in Santiago, he participated in preparatory meetings and helped set the Party up in Valparaiso, and therefore counted himself a founding member. After his release from prison shortly before the 1932 elections, he joined Marmaduke Grove's electoral campaign in Valparaiso where Grove won the highest number of votes of any candidate. Although Arturo Alessandri won the national elections,

Marmaduke Grove won the second highest number of votes overall, and his party got eight seats in parliament. Alessandri's election gradually brought to an end the chaotic period that had lasted since 1920. After 1933 the Chilean elite was forced to accept the inclusion of the organisations of the working class in the political system, although it did not completely abandon using repression. Having helped Grove's electoral campaign, Allende was able to return to his studies in time to finish his dissertation by the end of the year.

Allende's dissertation was titled 'Mental Hygiene and Crime' and was based in part on his work in the Santiago Psychiatric Hospital. His subject was chosen with a practical purpose in mind, to contribute to the improvement in the treatment of these illnesses received in Chile. Using the plural common at the time he wrote, 'We read, and the scientific exposition and the exact accounts of what has already been achieved in favour of this cause in other countries comforted our spirit. We observed, compared and lived our reality and were overcome by disappointment. [...] We were moved to [write the thesis] in the desire for better days, and with the memory of long hours of conversation in which criminals and delinquents opened the doorway of their intimate lives to us, spilling around us the blood, pain and misery-spattered source of their feelings.'[2] The description of one of Allende's case studies brings these words to life:

Name M.Z.C. 38 years of age. Father died of a cardiac seizure. He is an habitual alcoholic. Patient has been secluded in the insane asylum four times. Mother lives, she is ill and very nervous, she has had epileptic fits. Fourteen siblings, ten of whom died in early childhood. Another at the age of ten. The eldest was killed by M. The remaining brother is very weak. He cannot work and suffers from nervous afflictions.[3]

Such traumatic upbringings were shockingly common, and here we can glimpse why Allende had such a concern with infant mortality and what he later called the 'mother-child binary'. The study showed Allende's deep concern and empathy for the fate of the poor and the most vulnerable in society, but also his passion to find pragmatic and logical solutions to social problems. The thesis argued that, 'Yesterday's charity is today's social assistance. The collective need has overwhelmed [the possibilities of] personal kindness.' It was an early indication of his search for the solution of concrete and urgent problems.

The solutions Allende proposed bore much in common with his later legislative agenda. To overcome widespread alcohol abuse Allende recommended an education campaign and state control of distribution. With regard to tuberculosis he proposed the creation of a comprehensive public health system that would tackle the symptoms and the causes of the disease by dealing with diet, housing and education as well as provide hospitals, access to medicine and sanatoria. To deal with the venereal diseases affecting 20 per cent of the working population, he recommended a public information campaign in cinemas, factories and workplaces, and sexual education classes for both children and adults. With regard to the problem of drug use he observed that an international approach was needed, and that the production of drugs ought to be under state control. Allende also called for the creation of special establishments for the reclusion of drug addicts, recognising addiction as a form of illness, since it was wrong that 'these ill people be treated and attended to in the insane asylum as is the case today.' Allende also argued for penal reform along scientific lines ('it has been our lot to have a close acquaintance of our country's prison organisation' he wrote, no doubt recalling his own time behind bars). Prisons should separate prisoners according to the severity of their crimes, he argued, and they should receive treatment in order to promote their social reintegration. His thesis was clear evidence of how advanced his thinking was for the time, and of the dynamic relationship that existed between Allende's medical experiences, his political thinking and his practical mind-set. It was the first expression of something that remained key to his thinking for the rest of his life – socialism was the solution to the poverty, disease, crime and desperate insanity caused by 'over-exploitation' and deep structural socio-economic problems.

A few years later Allende developed some of the ideas presented in this thesis in 'Chile's Social-Medical Reality' published in 1940 after he had served as health minister in the

Popular Front government. The book described the shocking
state of healthcare in Chile, which he blamed on 'old economic
methods... based on free competition', and proposed a series
of measures based on cooperation and planning which would
restore the 'virility and health' of the working people to the
benefit of the national economy, and which would provide
'a better disposition and spirit to live and appreciate life.'[4] In
both texts, Allende developed his idea that the redistribution of
wealth and the rational re-ordering of society would resolve the
material, physical, psychological and spiritual problems faced
by the vast majority of Chileans.

Despite graduating with honours, Allende's entry into
professional life was not easy. He specifically chose to go into
public service, although it was not well paid and it exposed him
to political pressure. After graduating as a surgeon, Allende took
part in four public job competitions. Four times he won the
selection process, but had the job withdrawn at the last minute
because of his political activity. He eventually got a job as an
assistant in the morgue of the Van Buren Hospital in Valparaiso.
Here he did the work of three doctors, transferring, undressing,
cleaning and autopsying 1,500 bodies. Allende dealt with the
bodies of young and old, men and women, even abandoned
newborn babies – all bearing the signs of poverty, violence, illness
and misery. As he later said, 'I won my bread sticking my hands
in pus, cancers and death.'[5] It gave Allende first-hand knowledge
of poverty. He worked long days, beginning at 6 a.m. and often
ending at 10 p.m. When possible Allende continued his political
activity, attending Socialist Party meetings, or working in the
free 'Socialist Assistance' polyclinic.

The Socialist Party that Allende helped establish in Valparaiso
was founded by the fusion of several socialist groupings, among
them 'Socialist Revolutionary Action', the group that included
Allende's friends Marmaduke and Hugo Grove, as well as
several other influential freemasons. The elected leadership
of the new party included former anarchist Oscar Schnake
as General Secretary and Marmaduke Grove as 'Leader'. The
Socialist Party agreed to use a Marxism 'rectified and enriched
by all the scientific contributions of social progress' to interpret

reality, and recognised the need for class-based struggle. The Party envisioned the necessity of a 'Workers' dictatorship' in the transition from capitalism to socialism and it stated that an 'evolutionary transformation through the democratic system is not possible, because the dominant class has organised itself in corps of armed civilians and has established its own dictatorship in order to keep the workers in misery and in ignorance and impede their emancipation.' This was the origin of the Party's fickle and contradictory attitude towards electoral politics, which it was never able to adequately resolve.

The new Socialist Party (PS) had an internationalist outlook, and it proposed achieving the economic and political union of the peoples of Latin America, in order to arrive at a 'Federation of Socialist Republics' and the creation of an 'anti-imperialist economy'.[6] The socialists maintained a series of important differences with the Chilean Communist Party (PC), which they accused of being too heavily influenced by the Soviet Union. The Socialists did not see the Soviet Union as the bulwark of the global working class, and were critical of Stalin. The difference was a key factor in the establishment of the PS, which had a more nationalist and 'eminently Americanist' focus.[7] Allende shared these critiques and he always sought a Chilean solution to Chilean problems. However, he also recognised that the Chilean Communist Party also sought Chilean solutions to the nation's problems. This recognition formed the basis of Allende's and the Socialist Party's long cooperation with the PC.

The first members of the Socialist Party were from a wide variety of backgrounds unlike the Communist Party, which remained overwhelmingly proletarian until the 1960s. Some of its members had anarchist, radical, democrat or even communist backgrounds, or had been independent activists and agitators. Some were freemasons, others former members of the military, trade unionists, professionals and intellectuals. It was what the socialist historian Julio Cesar Jobet called 'a motley mass, tumultuous and impatient.'[8] Some saw the party as a 'true' communist party, striving to make it a working class vanguard, others as a platform for building a broad cross-class mass movement. The two visions would often come into conflict. In the late 1930s another element was added to the Party when Trotskyites expelled from the Communist Party joined it. The PS's heterogeneous composition was reflected in its politics and its structure, and meant that the Party tended towards '*caudillismo*' or the gravitation around popular chieftains within the Party. On the other hand its lack of ideological discipline meant that it was a relatively broad church and it was able to grow rapidly in its early years.

The union of these disparate socialist groupings was a big step forward for the Chilean left, creating a scenario where all those leftists that did not fit into the Communist mould could act within a political organisation that still acknowledged the need for a revolutionary transformation of society. The key to their success would lie in whether they would be able to cooperate effectively with the Communists in order to achieve their goals, and in this Salvador Allende would play a key role. Membership of any of the popular parties or trade unions was a mark of real commitment to the popular struggle. Left-wing activists risked repression, whether the constant threat of police, army or paramilitary militia violence, or the very real threat of losing a job and being blacklisted. At the same time this hardship created a palpable sense of solidarity and comradeship.

Throughout Latin America a repressive process had begun in response to the unrest provoked by the global economic crisis. In Brazil Getulio Vargas established his dictatorship, and Venezuela, Peru and Argentina also came under authoritarian rule. In El Salvador General Martinez destroyed a small Communist Party and massacred over 30,000 peasants. In Nicaragua Somoza consolidated his dictatorship after assassinating Augusto Sandino in 1933, and in the Dominican Republic Trujillo took power. Fearing 'Bolshevism', the United States backed these regimes, and in the wake of the 1930 economic crash built an economic system that used loans and bilateral agreements as indirect means of control, alongside an advantageous political system where the United States always dealt with weak Latin American countries bilaterally.[9]

Europe underwent a similar process of repression, with fascist regimes notoriously installed in Italy, Germany and much of

Southern and Eastern Europe. In response the Soviet Union pushed Communist Parties to begin creating 'Popular Front' governments of democratic forces in order to resist the fascist onslaught. In France and Spain Popular Front governments came to power, but one was ineffective and the other overthrown in a brutal and bloody civil war. The spectre of the Second World War loomed large. In Chile these global processes were reflected in Alessandri's repressive government, in threat of a Nazi takeover, and in the efforts by the Communist Party to create a Popular Front coalition that would include socialists, radicals and democrats.

Five days after the Socialist Party was founded Alessandri's government passed a law handing the president 'extraordinary powers' in order to deal with 'subversion'. Leaders of the new party were arrested, some forced into internal exile, others into hiding. As if the official repression was not enough, from 1935 Alessandri developed a 'Republican Militia', a civilian paramilitary army to repress left-wing organisations. Fascist right-wingers also created Nazi-style 'assault groups'. In response the Socialist Party created its own, albeit unarmed, militia. In these early days every Socialist Party member was expected to wear the militia uniform and be willing to combat the Republican and Nazi gangs. Mass street fights became common as the left sought to prevent fascist groups from organising openly. This was the environment in which Allende was formed as a Socialist Party leader, and one of the largest street battles involving hundreds of activists took place in Valparaiso.[10] A leader in organisation and in action, Allende was noted for his political activism and for his fighting skills. Allende later emphasised the importance of this period in the development of the Socialist Party, since this 'frontal struggle against nazi fascism' was not just 'the era of uniformed marches, of batons and nazi attacks against the workers' it was also a period of ideological struggle that helped the Party develop.[11] Allende may have also been recalling a notable period in his personal political development. Carlos Briones, a socialist from the Trotskyist wing of the Party and close friend, recalled that the Allende he met in 1936 did not yet have much 'clarity in Marxist thought', and was 'living

a process of theoretical definition'. In which Allende sought
to combine Marxism's scientific approach and its rationale for
revolution, with the anarchist ideas of his youth, and the liberal
and masonic ideas of his revered ancestors, in order to overcome
them with more 'progressive social thinking.'[12] It was a process
that took place in the midst of a heated and often violent social
struggle, and in close contact with the poor of Valparaiso. It
was around this time, in 1935, that in recognition of his ability
and leadership, Allende was elected Regional Secretary of the
Socialist Party in Valparaiso.

Figure 3.1   Salvador Allende in his Socialist militia uniform.

Meanwhile the Alessandri government continued its barely
concealed dictatorship, maintaining favourable policies for US
companies and cracking down on the political opposition. An
indigenous people's revolt in the south was crushed with great
brutality and over 300 people killed.[13] The massacre caused great
upset as it followed the brutal crushing of a railway workers'
strike earlier in the year. As a well-known socialist leader in
Valparaiso, Salvador Allende was sent into internal exile to the

small fishing village of Caldera some 600 miles north of the capital. Characteristically Allende did not remain idle. During his six-month sentence he provided free medical care to the locals and their families, vaccinating them, teaching the rudiments of maternal and infant healthcare, as well as giving political talks and founding the area's first Socialist Party section. For a long time afterwards the area remained a left-wing redoubt. The Socialist Party protested his exile, and in Santiago Marmaduke Grove raised the issue in the Senate putting Allende's name on the national agenda for the first time.

Shortly before his exile to Caldera, Allende was put forward for membership of the 4th 'Progress' Lodge of the Chilean Freemasons by its Venerable Master his good friend Jorge Grove. Allende was attracted by its philosophy that aimed to 'sweep away ignorance, overcome obscurantism' and create 'a regime of equality of rights and expectations for all men', as well as by his family history of freemasonry. In a country where many leading figures in business and politics were freemasons – among them Marmaduke Grove, the leader of the Socialist Party – membership could also open doors to a politically minded and ambitious young man, and in mid 1935 Allende indicated his willingness to join.[14] Despite his distinguished family background, Allende's politics were controversial and sparked an intense debate which was only resolved after an investigation. The Masonic report on Allende stated that he had 'a very superior intellect' and 'great character'. It noted that he had volunteered for military service and that he had a sober lifestyle 'correspondent with his age.' His honour was considered untainted. As a result his candidacy was approved. He was initiated on the evening of the 18 November 1935, shortly after his return from Caldera. As part of his initiation Allende had to respond in writing to three questions. The surviving record of the questions and his answers shows the maturity that Allende's thought had already achieved:

- What duties does a man have towards his fellow men?
  - Man is only a part of the social whole; therefore his life should be at its service, that is, at the service of his fellow men.

- What duties does he have towards himself?
  - That of organising his existence in accordance with a clear conception of his obligations, duties and rights, which are subject to the duties and rights of everyone else.
- What memory of yourself would you like to leave for posterity?
  - That of having fulfilled the obligation I gave myself of having been useful to society, pushing each day for the spiritual, moral and material perfection of society.[15]

Although initially being a freemason may have assisted in Allende's rapid rise to prominence, it soon caused him problems when a rightward turn in the Socialist Party leadership sparked a debate among the rank and file on whether the freemasonry was causing the party to deviate from its revolutionary politics, and again when the party became more doctrinaire during the 1960s. In the wake of the Cuban revolution, many freemasons also found it increasingly difficult to sympathise with Allende's political project. Yet Allende never renounced his membership, although by the late 1960s he was no longer very active.

Apart from its practical appeal, for Allende freemasonry had 'a great and sublime mission' to promote among its members the need for them to define, 'using modern standards', the principles of Liberty, Equality and Fraternity, in order to create a society free of 'alienation, unemployment, low wages and preventable diseases' through the creation of a 'well-functioning and efficient social security system' that would open 'the broad roads of culture' to all.[16] Allende constantly encouraged the Freemasons to adopt this vision of their mission, and to include more working class members, more young intellectuals, and to become more democratic. Allende the newly-initiated Freemason dived straight back into his political activity. He founded the Chilean College of Medicine, and began editing its bulletin in 1936. In recognition of his work in organising the Socialist Party in Valparaiso and Caldera the Party put him forward as congressional candidate for Quillota and Valparaiso in 1936. He was also elected Deputy General Secretary of the Socialist Party in 1937.

Allende won his seat in Valparaiso, as well as contributing to the victory of three other socialists in the city. It was part of an impressive showing – in four short years the Party had established a national presence with just over 11 per cent of the national vote. Allende soon developed a reputation as a pugnacious parliamentarian, who, as a Peruvian friend later recalled, tended to 'unequivocal and sharp responses to impertinence'.[17] It was part of a harsher side of his character, an intolerance of what he perceived as mediocrity or dishonourable behaviour. Yet Allende was not generally intolerant, and his friends and collaborators recall a man who distinguished between adversaries and enemies, and who once said 'I am passionate and violent in the defence of my ideas, my principles, of the party doctrine that I sustain, but I have never made it personal.'[18]

In one of his early speeches in Congress, Allende critiqued a government healthcare bill arguing that only socialism could adequately resolve Chile's problems. Allende argued that poverty and lack of healthcare caused Chile's horrific mortality and infant mortality rates of 26.8 per 1,000 inhabitants, and 238 per 1,000 births, respectively. Allende described how 53 per cent of hospitals had no children's wards and none had central heating. Furthermore, social insurance only covered 13 per cent of the population. Allende described how 87 per cent of working people's salaries went on food, clothing and heating. He described how Chileans ate only 30 per cent of what was then considered normal. 'It isn't possible to allow an entire people to continue to be starved', he exclaimed. Starvation was exacerbated by lack of clothing and shelter; 'there are innumerable sick people that arrive at hospitals who only need warmth and shelter', he said. In order to remedy the chronic shortage of decent housing, he argued for the construction of 300,000 new homes. Allende criticised the government's proposed legislation since it showed 'no leadership, no systematisation' and was underfunded. The legislation did not provide for an integrated system and did not contemplate tackling the fundamental cause of ill health – poverty – which could only be tackled in a 'controlled, planned, socialised economy... in which the anarchy of today, which allows the few to live at the expense of the many, can be overcome.'[19] In his four-year career as a parliamentary deputy Allende presented bills on the education of workers and peasants, the prohibition of monopolies, reforms to the Labour Code, and the creation of the Supreme Council for the Protection of Children and Adolescents, demonstrating his consistent concern with the practical concerns of working people.

Shortly after Allende's election the Radicals and the Socialists agreed, with communist encouragement, to present a unitary Popular Front candidate in the 1938 presidential elections. The candidate chosen was the radical Pedro Aguirre Cerda, whose slogan was 'to govern is to educate'. The road to the Popular Front was not easy. The left was divided. Street fights between communists, Trotskyists and socialists were common. Many socialists opposed an alliance with sectors they considered bourgeois and potentially treacherous. They therefore had a policy of a United Workers' Front, excluding any bourgeois party. In the vigorous internal debate on the Popular Front, Allende supported Grove and Oscar Schnake in backing an alliance with the Communists and Radicals, a posture that eventually won out. Allende and those like him thought that bringing the Radicals into government would mean an advance since it would bring 'the petit-bourgeoisie into the exercise of power'. However, Allende was also aware that despite being a big step forward the Popular Front was also a coalition dominated by the Radicals, who would therefore dominate economic policy. According to Allende 'the Popular Front did not imply and could not imply political liberation and full sovereignty' and therefore 'we consciously acted within the Popular Front as a stage [of political development]'.[20]

Even within the Communist Party there were those who mistrusted Aguirre Cerda who had been a minister under Alessandri. However, with their policy now officially supported by the Third International, the Communists were vigorous in building the Popular Front with allies in the Radical and Socialist parties. Meanwhile the Radicals, who had spent much of the 1920s and 1930s see-sawing between opposition and government, were feeling pressured on the left by the energetic and popular Socialist Party, but were also incensed by the brutal repression of civil liberties under Alessandri. For all three groupings the alliance had its advantages and the Popular Front began to take shape with Socialist and Communist support for a victorious Radical candidate in an April 1936 by-election showing how effective the new coalition could be. Then the socialist, anarcho-syndicalist and communist trade union federations united in December 1936 in the Confederation of Workers of Chile (CTCH, Confederacion de Trabajadores de Chile), proclaiming their support for the Popular Front. This historic unity soon brought them the reward of electoral victory, but the parties that came to form the Popular Front still contested the 1937 parliamentary elections separately.

The October 1938 Presidential election was the first to be fought in Chile on an explicit left–right split. The left campaigned on the slogan 'Bread, Roof and Clothing', the right on 'Order and Work'. The limitations of Chile's democracy were a significant challenge to the aspirations of the Popular Front. Of the population of 5 million people only 500,000 could legally vote, a circumstance that clearly benefitted the right. Furthermore, the right habitually used underhand tactics to get votes – from bribery and blackmail to the '*encerrona*' practice of locking people that might vote for the left in their workplaces until the polling stations closed. The parties of the left used a variety of methods to counter this. Socialist students went out to rural areas to invigilate the voting process. Others even used home made tear gas grenades while fighting the thugs protecting the '*encerronas*' where working people were corralled.[21] This combative stance was key in allowing a democratic electoral result. Despite widespread fraud, a weighted electoral system, and a propaganda campaign mounted by the right, the Popular Front candidate, Pedro Aguirre Cerda, won. As in Allende's victory 32 years later, Aguirre Cerda's was statistically narrow, and some elements of the right tried to claim that the result was illegitimate. As in 1970 the distortions of the electoral system hid a much broader level of support.

As Allende stated during the Valparaiso campaign, 'The Popular Front government cannot be confused with a socialist government. The "Frontist" government has been created to defend the democratic guarantees against the shadowy threat of fascism'.[22] There was no question of profoundly changing the existing socio-economic order. Accordingly, the communists did not claim any ministerial posts so as to maintain the support of right-wing sectors in the Radical Party and to avoid provoking a coup as had occurred in Spain, but the new cabinet included several socialist ministers, including a youthful Salvador Allende as Health Minister.

Soon after the Popular Front took power Chile was shaken by a ferocious earthquake which struck the city of Chillan on 25 January 1939. The city was completely destroyed. Tens of thousands of people perished. In the aftermath of the earthquake Allende rushed to the scene in order to help organise the relief effort. Chile did not have a public emergency service, so it was down to the public, and civil society organisations together with the army and police, to organise the emergency relief. The Socialist Militia were mobilised and provided immediate assistance, rescuing survivors and clearing rubble. Allende himself provided medical care to some victims. To help rebuild after the earthquake the Popular Front government created the National Corporation for the Promotion of Production (CORFO). This organisation played an important role in Chile's subsequent economic development, substituting for non-existent national private investment in industry and strategic sectors of the economy. The CORFO created a steel industry, a plan for the electrification of the country, a system of loans for agricultural producers, all with the intention of creating the basis for development. As one Chilean economist later put it 'the industrialisation and modernisation of the country was owed almost exclusively to state intervention, since the state had to take on the role of entrepreneur as a result of the weakness or lack of interest of the private sector.'[23] The government also pushed hard to improve and expand the education system, under the slogan 'to govern is to educate'. 385,000 children were brought into primary education, and the state founded vocational schools designed to create a qualified workforce. Together they were the Popular Front's most lasting legacy.

At the time of the earthquake Allende was attending a Masonic meeting in central Santiago. While out on the street after having fled the building, Allende bumped into a friend who was accompanied by Hortensia Bussi. Despite her criticising Allende's masonic membership the two began their romance shortly afterwards. One of the things she recalled attracting her was the way he described the tragedies of the disaster zone with deep empathy for its victims.[24] Within a few months 'Tencha', as she was known, fell pregnant. Under some pressure from friends and relatives, the couple married in a civil ceremony in Santiago on 17 September 1939. Tencha herself later recalled the wedding occurred without a party or invitations, partly because of Salvador's ministerial workload, but also because 'we weren't a traditional couple.'[25] The newlyweds moved into a building just by the Santa Lucia hill, sharing residence with a number of notable political figures, including Romulo Betancourt, later President of Venezuela who was then in exile in Chile. Betancourt shared a love of boxing with Allende, and soon became a regular sparring partner. The central location in a distinguished neighbourhood allowed Allende to mix his work and social life. Each morning Allende rose and did exercises before heading to work. After work Allende attended meetings, or conversed long hours in café's or friends' homes, mixing with politicians, Peruvian exiles and with the young socialists that he grouped around himself.

In September 1939, thanks to his work on Aguirre Cerda's campaign, Allende was appointed Health Minister. Allende developed the project of a National Plan for the Defence of Public Health, which became the social and human development arm of the government's programme. As Allende later explained, measures to improve public health would only work if supported by economic and financial measures that increased the overall standard of living. The Plan called for the allocation of US$20 million to fund new hospitals, polyclinics, psychiatric institutions, a cancer institute, the construction of waste burning facilities, sewerage works, increased funding for laboratories at the University of Chile, improved facilities for mothers and children and a raft of measures designed to improve the supply of drugs (which were mostly imported from Europe and therefore in short supply thanks to the war). Peasants were to be given small loans in order to help boost milk production, and each province was to receive a pasteurisation facility to process it. Together with the measures envisioned for the CORFO, Allende said the National Health Plan represented 'the most serious steps yet taken in defence of the human economy, in defence of human capital, that we consider the source of all wealth and the base of all progress.'[26] The legislation was approved albeit with serious modifications which changed the substance of the reforms, but it was still a big advance.

During this period Allende proposed many other bills that showed his, and the Socialist Party's, interest in gaining sovereignty over Chile's natural resources, and improving the lives of Chile's people. One concern was with the poor state of Chile's housing, and in 1940 he demonstrated his flair for publicity by organising a National Housing Conference, where he had examples of poor people's huts erected in front of the Union Club where the Chilean oligarchy met. During the same week, a team of six workers built a decent, fully equipped home right next to them, showing that it was possible to resolve Chile's housing problems.

Within the Socialist Party, participation in the Popular Front government had been controversial from the beginning. Being in government meant many compromises, particularly since the Radical Party dominated the coalition. Furthermore, once the Second World War began in Europe, the United States became the only source of available credit and machinery, forcing the government to alter its National Development Plan to benefit the private sector. This change led to problems within the Socialist Party and the Popular Front. In August 1940 Oscar Schnake travelled to the United States to negotiate loan conditions, and returned in December pushing for the Communists to be expelled from the Popular Front, going against the will of the majority of the membership.[27] This exacerbated already serious problems between socialists and communists thanks to the assassination of Trotsky in Mexico earlier that year, and the Communist position supporting neutrality in the war. Despite this, in March 1941

Figure 3.2   Salvador Allende as Minister of Health during the 19 September military parade of 1940, together with the Minister of Work, Juan Praderas Munoz.

elections were held in which the PS polled 17 per cent of the vote and the PC 12 per cent. Both parties were now undoubtedly major players in Chilean politics. However the conflict between them sharpened, with the Socialist Interior Minister closing the Communist newspaper, *El Siglo*, because of its 'anti-Americanism'. Along with internal debates in the Radical Party this infighting weakened the government and contributed to the dilution of its economic and social programmes.

The stance of the leadership, the slow pace of change and the dilution of reforms disillusioned many Socialists, and a debate began on whether the Party ought to remain in government. In 1940 some left to form the Socialist Workers' Party (PST). Then Pedro Aguirre Cerda died of tuberculosis in November 1941, forcing fresh elections to be held. The Socialist Party put forward its own candidate, Oscar Schnake, but he was soundly beaten by Juan Antonio Rios, the candidate of a fresh alliance of Radicals, the PST and Communists. Although Rios pledged to continue the process of reforms, the Socialist Party fell victim to bitter infighting, officially leaving the government although its ministers, including Allende, remained in post. In power, Rios began to retreat on many issues and he even began to repress the left. Shortly afterwards, in February 1942, Salvador Allende resigned from the government. With his Party in crisis Allende decided to stand for the leadership, competing with his old friend and mentor, Marmaduke Grove, who wanted the Socialists to support the Rios government. In January 1943 Allende was elected General Secretary of the Socialist Party. Grove resigned and formed a breakaway party. The Party was disintegrating under pressure.

Allende was seen as the candidate who could put the Socialist Party back on course, popular among the leadership and the membership of the party.[28] In August 1943 he presided over an Extraordinary Congress that was held in his hometown, Valparaiso. Allende sought to clarify and resolve the Party's internal problems, while identifying lessons to be learned from its first experience of government. In his opening speech Allende described the political situation, and then commenced an extraordinary critique of the PS itself, 'Perhaps I do not faithfully interpret the thought of my comrades, I take personal responsibility for this', he began. He accused the Party of failing to understand its past, criticising its lack of political understanding. 'The Party', he said, 'has not been a school by socialists for socialists', it lacked 'philosophical and social preparation', and the lack of a uniform doctrine meant 'the militants do not separate doctrine from tactics or political line.' This made it extremely difficult to adopt a coherent political line, because it was always thought to be in violation of the Party's doctrine.

Allende also identified organisational failures and a culture of individualism, gossip and slander within the Party. 'In the past we had incorporated the old anarchist principle 'an offence against one is an offence against all'. 'Now', Allende said, insults were the subject of gossip. Allende also criticised the democratic excesses that had led to disciplinary chaos. Local and regional leaders were able to distort internal elections and then do what they wanted, even if it violated Party policy. This *caudillismo* needed to be overcome: 'We don't ask or demand respect for the man, but for the role he carries out', Allende remarked.

Allende identified the lack of a programme as the Party's greatest fault saying, 'Our philosophy is Marxism enriched by experience, but we have no programme.' He continued, 'We need to give the Party a uniform, homogenous, and compact orientation.' Such a programme had to take into account that 'tactics change according to reality, and this demands that the political line, or the tactics, be changed to fit that reality.' It was a criticism of the Party's dogmatism. 'This Congress', Allende continued, 'could be the starting point of a new life. Let's take advantage of our past experiences, let's keep making stark and hard criticisms of ourselves'. The Party had to move from standing together to having a flexible ideological unity that he called 'unity of thought'. Almost as if he knew that his speech would be badly received he ended saying, 'Comrade delegates, you will decide.'[29]

Allende did not give up trying to get his comrades to be less dogmatic. In a courageous move, a few months after the Valparaiso Congress Allende organised a demonstration to pay homage to the Popular Front government that the Socialists had recently left. Allende emphasised the successful measures undertaken by the Popular Front and claimed them for the PS. In effect he was trying to make its members understand that while the Popular Front had indeed become a 'left-wing government with a right-wing economic system' it had also fought and won many battles against the elite.[30] Therefore it could not be disowned or denigrated. Allende praised the Popular Front for beginning a new stage in Chilean history that had brought the left into power, and showed that it could make a real difference to the lives of ordinary people.

During 1943, while Allende was General Secretary of the PS, the leadership of the Communist Party proposed that the two parties should merge in order to unite the parties of the working class. The dissolution of the Comintern in May that year seemed to eliminate one of the major problems between the two organisations. However, as Allende argued in a letter to the Communist General Secretary, the Socialist Party, while agreeing to the idea in principle, had strong reservations. Allende argued that unification had to be the result of a process and not the beginning. There were still many knotty issues of difference. The PS asked the Communists to define their position on the unification of Latin America, since, as Allende wrote to Carlos Contreras, 'only a united and firm Latin America will be heard in the future peace.' Then Allende wrote 'the Communist Party has proposed the "National Unity" [alliance with the Radicals] as the solution to Chile's problems. We cannot accept a policy of this type. The great problems of today demand more than ever a clear definition that allows people to have an orientation, to act within its postulates and in accordance with the economic solutions that these determine.' Thus the two parties continued to have differences too deep to unite, but the PS did 'esteem it convenient that the country know that socialists and communists are ready to join a common electoral struggle.'[31] For Allende, it seemed, the socialists had to become a little more like the communists, and the communists a little more like the socialists.

In 1944 Allende was put forward as a senatorial candidate for the south of Chile, from the lakes region down to Tierra del Fuego. Recognising that much of the nearer reaches of the region were dominated by right-wing landowners, he concentrated on the far south, on Tierra del Fuego, where the PS had identified a large working class of shepherds, meat packers, and port and agricultural labourers. The region also had a history of strong leftist activism that went back to the arrival of Communards fleeing France in the 1870s.[32] Allende travelled the length and breadth of the isolated and undeveloped region, spending much of the time on horseback, reaching out to rural communities. He won the election and in March 1945 he became one of two Socialist Party senators. Meanwhile Allende's party was exhausted by its internal struggles and disputes with the Communists. In the March 1945 elections it polled 12.7 per cent, down from over 17 per cent in 1941. Meanwhile the Communist Party maintained its showing (despite remaining illegal and having to campaign under another name), gaining over 10 per cent. Shortly after this election, and thanks to his unpopular criticisms, Allende was voted off the Socialist Party leadership, and he was never again to hold Party office.

The following year, Chile held Presidential elections. The PS put forward its own candidate, who polled 2.53 per cent. The communists supported the Radical candidate Gabriel Gonzalez Videla, who won. Then in the April 1947 municipal elections the Communists polled nearly 17 per cent, confirming themselves as a major political presence. The socialists remained hostile to the government, and to their erstwhile allies. However, while the electoral pact with the Radicals succeeded for the third time, the communists' faith in Gonzalez Videla could not take into account changes in the international situation. In Europe, with the Second World War over, the chills of the Cold War began to replace the warmth of wartime cooperation. In Greece Communist partisans were crushed with US and UK support. In Italy, France and Belgium the main concern of the Western allies became preventing communists from dominating the post-war situation. In Latin America, under US pressure, communists became the target of renewed repression in order to 'protect' democracy.[33]

Unlike the over-optimistic communists, Allende and the Socialist Party thought that although the Second World War had changed the world, competition between the victors was inevitable. While the war had destroyed fascism and created an alliance between the Anglo-Saxon powers and the Soviet Union, and had forced immense socio-economic changes on the United Kingdom and the United States, Allende foresaw that potential Soviet domination of Europe would lead the Western Allies to seek to neutralise it by looking to their own areas of domination. For Britain that meant strengthening the Empire; for the United States it meant 'seeking the support of its satellites in Latin America'.[34] Latin American support was not just necessary in the new United Nations, but also to allow continued cheap access to vital raw materials. In effect, the nations of Latin America were to provide the materials that financed the Marshall Plan for Europe. Therefore, the renewed repression of the communists was not entirely surprising. The virulent anti-communist fears of the Chilean oligarchy were now allied to that of the US government and US corporations. The three would from now on fight together to contain what they saw as the communist menace.

In Chile the immediate effect was that the communists began to be pushed out of government they had helped elect. The three communist ministers were expelled from cabinet and in September 1948 the Party was proscribed. Its members were erased from the electoral rolls, sacked from government jobs, and its leaders sent to concentration camps in the northern desert. Some high profile members sought exile, among them Pablo Neruda, Chile's future Nobel prize-winner. For Salvador Allende and for the Chilean Socialists it was now time to decide whose side they would stand on. With government encouragement some leading socialists opposed any alliance with the communists.[35] Allende and the majority that believed in the unity of the working class, were forced to set up a new party called the Popular Socialist Party (PSP). The PSP was to be the cradle of most of the Socialist leaders of the Popular Unity. The pre-war cooperation in the Popular Front, the Socialist's traditional independence from international groupings, alongside the Party's Marxist philosophy ensured that at this crucial point most of them refused to abandon their fellow revolutionaries.

Salvador Allende vigorously opposed the anti-communist repression in one of his greatest speeches where he denounced the 'Law for the Permanent Defence of Democracy' as a 'veritable atomic bomb fallen in the midst of our social coexistence'. In this speech he defended the communists' Marxist ideology, and appealed to the democratic instincts of his fellow Senators, underlining the importance of freedom of expression and association, and pointed out that socio-economic misery and imperialist exploitation made the communists' struggle legitimate. Allende also foresaw that the law could, 'tomorrow, easily be applied to us, who are doctrinally Marxists and revolutionaries'. For Allende, the law put Chile's entire political system at risk, and was potentially the first step on the slippery slope to dictatorship.

Allende outlined the failures of Chile's existing democracy, saying that 'the freedom of today's social organisation is just for show, only a small minority of those who control power and the means of production is in reality free'. But he also recognised 'with a strict sense of realism' the impossibility of socialism in Chile – 'for now'. It was because of this that the socialists respected and strove to improve Chile's 'bourgeois democracy'. 'We will always act within legal channels, while the democratic regime respects the vote, trade union and social rights, and the guarantees of our Founding Document: freedom of thought, of association and of the press.' Allende condemned the cynicism of those who accused the Communists of 'Soviet imperialism', yet had nothing to say about US imperialism whose effects directly affected Chile. Allende cited the injustice of the US-fixed Metal Reserve prices that forced Chile to sell copper and other raw materials to the United States at a low price, amounting to a loss for Chile of some US$500 million.[36]

Allende also appealed to the Radical government of the day, recalling his Radical grandfather's words: 'the struggle of [political] parties [...] is great and beautiful, whereas the government which tries to be sectarian is small-minded and worthy of damnation.' At the same time he reminded them that his grandfather had himself been condemned for being 'red'. He summarised the philosophical basis of Marxism, and how it shaped his concept of socialist revolution, establishing Marxism as the inheritor of liberal, rational and materialist thought going back to Democritus and Heraclitus. He thus implied that socialists, communists, radicals, liberals and democrats shared a philosophical ancestry and a concern with democracy. Yet, he argued, those who sought to proscribe the Communist Party did not understand democracy, 'democracy, well understood, is the possibility of rebellion against injustice, the chance of fulfilment, it is a spiritual attitude of constant improvement. Democracy, Mr President, is a conscious result arrived at through principles, ideas, and doctrines, and not with police measures.' Allende then described how a democratic transformation would be truly revolutionary, arriving at his first public expression of his later political practice – 'He who manages to achieve power temporarily by force is not revolutionary. On the other hand, a governor, who manages to transform society, social coexistence and the economic basis of the country [after] arriving to power legally, can be revolutionary. That is the sense that we give to the concept of revolution – profound and creative transformation.' The revolution was thus something that other political groups could share in, something that also belonged to them. For Allende, although the Popular Front was now dead, its successes had indicated that a peaceful revolution was possible, that Chilean institutions were flexible enough to change their purpose and sustain a process of radical change. It was a vision to which he held firm for the rest of his life. Furthermore, even though it had now been defeated, it had left behind a legacy that shaped Chile through to 1973 and beyond. A vivid demonstration of what the peaceful road could achieve.

Allende finished his speech by roundly condemning the proposal to ban the Communist Party: 'This law goes against the Constitution' and it 'attacks the very basis of the democratic regime.'[37] Despite his argument the law was passed and the Communist Party made illegal. Ironically, four months later the government gave women the vote, unless of course they were communists. The passing of what the Communists called the 'Damned Law' marked the end of the Popular Front governments and the internationalisation of the Cold War logic that would increasingly dominate Chile. For Allende it marked the completion of a process of ideological development in which he came to envision a peaceful revolution, a 'Chilean road to socialism, as well as the moment that foreign intervention became a fundamental enemy of Chilean independence.

4

Becoming the Leader of the Left

At the moment of the death of the Popular Front there came a pause. The Communist Party was banned, the Socialist Party divided, and their erstwhile Radical allies in government with the enemy. The unity of the trade union movement was also in tatters. The left's immediate task was to rebuild unity, and their mass movement. It was a task that Allende would contribute greatly to. Allende was now the father of three daughters, Isabel, Carmen Paz and Beatriz. He had a small circle of close collaborators, to which a new and important addition arrived in 1950. Miguel Labarca, a fellow student activist of the 1920s had been in exile in Europe and Argentina since the early 1940s. Upon his return he encountered what he considered a far more developed proletariat, and an Allende who had achieved 'full maturity of thought, faith in himself and a definitive aplomb.' Allende was giving a speech at a copper workers' strike, and Labarca heard him speak about the impossibility of social development under capitalism for the peoples of the Third World. 'There is underdevelopment because there is imperialism, and there is imperialism because there is underdevelopment', Allende said. Labarca agreed. Labarca, a fellow freemason, was an irascible intellectual on whom Allende came to rely for political advice.

Labarca joined the group of leftists that worked alongside Allende. Such group work had characterised Allende since the mid 1930s, perhaps a habit picked up from his medical work. Throughout his mature life Allende gathered groups of leftists around him, mostly young politically independent males with a commitment to his vision of the road to socialism. Unafraid of the brilliance of others, each decade furnished him with a new group of collaborators, who joined previous generations and assisted him in his research, in his fundraising and with whatever needed doing. Labarca was soon helping Allende improve his oratory by learning from nineteenth century British Prime Minister, Benjamin Disraeli, who adapted his tone and style to his audience.

This effort to improve was a constant feature of Allende's life. Back in 1939, when he became Health Minister, Allende had sought to learn to control his temper, 'the irresistible compulsion to react with violence to impertinence', which had been a necessary characteristic on the combative streets of the 1930s – an effort he largely succeeded in, possibly by learning to meditate.[1] It was demonstrative of Allende's belief in 'mind over matter', for as he told Osvaldo Puccio, one of his young collaborators in 1951, 'The body obeys the instructions of the brain, one can order the body to do whatever the brain wants. It is a question of having the will to do so.' This attitude meant Allende was capable of immense hard work, and by the 1950s Allende was squeezing '30 hours into a 24 hour day', waking early, exercising and waking friends and colleagues with 6 a.m. phone calls.[2] At the same time Allende did not neglect the body, reputedly eating an apple a day, which he peeled with a pocket knife leaving a single coil of peel.

During the early 1950s Senator Allende had a small office in the Congress building in central Santiago. Allende had a constant stream of petitioners and visitors, and Allende eventually had the room divided by a wooden partition screen. Allende requested that the Senate press office send him press cuttings on issues that interested him and together with his team he used these to develop ideas, and illustrate his speeches. His constant need for data also led him to promote the work of the Library of Congress, eventually enabling it to become one of the most important social science collections in Latin America. The office was in no way secure, but Allende laughed off adopting any security measures, arguing that they would be too much bother and their absence would keep them honest.[3]

An established politician, Allende now lived a comfortable middle class existence with his wife, three daughters and a dog called 'Chagual'. The couple were given a loan and they bought a small house in Providencia, a well-to-do but accessible area of Santiago. He returned home for lunch most days, usually with guests. In the evenings his collaborators often gathered in his red and gold-carpeted study to work on speeches or proposals. Well-equipped with books and a comfortable sofa and seats, Allende's study was watched over by a large portrait of his grandfather, Ramon Allende Padin, and was notable in that it lacked a desk. People wrote with pads or typewriters perched on their laps, or brought in what the Allende's called a 'bridge table'. Work would proceed overseen by the signed photographs of revolutionary leaders and cultural figures from across the world on the shelves of a floor to ceiling bookcase on one wall.[4]

Figure 4.1   The Allende Bussi family on the terrace of their house in Guardia Vieja, together with their dog, Chagual.

However, with the left and its unions in disarray money was short. Allende was forced to undertake business ventures that might help finance his political campaigns. One involved bringing US-style milk bars to Chile, another a factory to make fish powder. Both were quite successful and were later sold off. Allende also bought a small house in the seaside village of Algarrobo, which soon developed into a highly fashionable beach resort. Here he would often take his daughters and friends sailing in a small dinghy.

In early 1951, with Presidential elections looming, the PSP leadership agreed to conversations with Carlos Ibañez, the former dictator, who had been elected senator in 1945, and who was in the process of a 'democratic cleansing' of his name. Allende firmly opposed any alliance with a man he characterised as a kind of fascist, and who had brutally repressed the left during his 1927–31 dictatorship. Despite his opposition, the PSP continued to work with Ibañez, and Allende resigned from the Party. Shortly afterwards he joined the Socialist Party of Chile. This faction, led by a small group of anti-communist Socialists had progressively lost influence since 1947. Allende was undoubtedly a heavyweight political figure in comparison to its leaders, and he soon turned it on its head, allying it with the Communist Party.

Meanwhile the Communist Party was operating underground, but it still had a national organisation and was capable of backing a nationwide electoral campaign. It was a marriage of both convenience and ideology. For the communists, Allende was a man who could be trusted, with his consistent defence of a strategic alliance with their Party and his eloquent rejection of the 'Damned Law'. For Allende, the communists represented both an electoral base and an essential component of any revolutionary process, 'they are the party of the working class', he told Osvaldo Puccio in early 1950, 'whoever wants to form a socialist government without the communists isn't a Marxist'.[5]

The new alliance was dubbed the Frente del Pueblo (People's Front), and Allende became its candidate in November 1951. This was his first presidential campaign. It was under-resourced, and much of the left's support had been repressed into silence or had leached away to Carlos Ibañez's populist campaign. Volodia Teitelboim, Allende's election secretary, later recalled, 'We felt a feeling of loneliness. The repression had taken its toll. The people were in retreat. The old organisation had been dispersed. We had to start again, and that's what we began.'[6]

With scant financial resources the campaign consisted of a small group of companions, usually Allende, the aged

Communist leader Elias Lafferte and a few others travelling in Allende's personal car if close enough to Santiago, or in a small Cessna piloted by a friend of Allende's if further away. Standing on soapboxes, Allende's comrades would gather a small crowd before Allende addressed them. His speeches, as Miguel Labarca recalled, were didactic and 'not distinguished by brevity'.[7] Allende would explain the national and international situation, and place it within the context of Chile's historical development, insisting that the people had to unite in order to undertake a leading role. One youth, who later became Allende's personal secretary, recalled a meeting in the northern city of Antofagasta. The crowd first sang the national anthem, left fists clenched in the air. Then 'The Internationale' and the socialist 'Marseillaise'. After warm-up speeches Allende rose to speak. 'The man captivated me from his first words', Agnic recalled. 'He spoke of things I had lived in my own flesh during my time in Chuquicamata [the famous copper mine]', 'It was like listening to a professor give a masterclass.' Allende spoke a little about his life, and explained how Chile's socio-economic inequalities were caused, and how the elite acted to protect its interests through the political right.'[8] Allende's first campaign lasted 283 days, using the slogan 'The people to victory with Allende!'

A close atmosphere characterised the campaign. Despite the difficulties and the small crowds, Allende never lost his enthusiasm or sense of humour. He insisted that the speakers had to include irrelevant words or phrases in the midst of their speeches, with failure punished by donation to the campaign fund. Carmen Lazo, a companion on the 1952 campaign trial also recalled Allende tying knots in the sleeves of her nightdress. 'He would shriek with laughter when I chased him', she remembered.[9] On their car journeys Allende, while driving at breakneck speed, would share sips of whisky, and the travellers would recite poetry and sing songs. The campaign was punctuated by events that underlined the seriousness of their task. On one journey in the north the car was signalled to halt by a waving torchlight. A woman's voice came out of the darkness, 'we want to speak to Doctor Allende'. It was a group of nitrate workers who had been hounded out of their jobs, and who had scrabbled together some money for Allende's campaign. On another trip Allende's group met with undercover trade union leaders, who were being illegally persecuted by bosses in an American-owned mining company. It must have made clear the complete absence of Chilean sovereignty in the foreign-owned enclaves, and the tremendous responsibility that Allende had to defend those with no voice.

It was during the 1952 campaign that one of the picaresque episodes of Allende's life occurred. Allende was challenged to a duel by a fellow senator and old schoolfriend, Raul Rettig. For many years it was thought the duel was over an insult, but shortly before his death Rettig explained that it was over a woman, Leonor Benavides, a former adolescent sweetheart of Allende's and his then passion.[10] Allende's comrades were aghast at what they considered his frivolity. His communist allies despaired at what they considered a 'bourgeois affectation'. Allende responded by saying that he had to act in a society of bourgeois values and that if he allowed an insult to pass, his image would be fatally undermined.[11] Given the cause this was doubtful, but the duel duly took place with both shots missing. It was testament to Allende's old-fashioned sense of honour, and his political nous. In 1952 he was the candidate of a small, underfunded campaign facing an uphill battle. He needed to seize some limelight, and the duel briefly brought him some attention.

The 1952 elections were the first in which Chilean women could vote. Allende's politics had always been marked by a concern for women and children as the most vulnerable sectors of society, and Allende therefore formed a women's committee in his campaign. Other committees considered the economy, foreign affairs and Chile's various social problems. In this organisation Allende was ahead of his time. Nobody had previously sought to examine the full spectrum of problems facing the nation using scientific data and internationally recognised indices. As well as providing him with the information he needed, over the years these teams helped to create a corps of social scientists with the knowledge and experience to administer the key sectors of the economy in the future. Allende's campaign was the antithesis of Ibañez's populist simplicity. It mattered little. Ibañez won the elections and an Ibañista mob attacked Allende's campaign offices. Allende returned to his duties in the Senate. He had polled only 5.6 per cent of the vote, but the campaign had placed Allende on the national stage for the first time. The 1952 elections marked the beginning of the long road to the unity of the left, and marked Allende out as a future contender.

During the early 1950s Allende was heavily involved in pushing for more state control over Chile's US-dominated copper industry. Despite providing 65 per cent of the national income the industry was in the hands of three US companies. To make matters worse, the state had no expertise on the copper industry or the world copper market. Allende protested that this situation was 'a crime against the nation'.[12] Allende was also offended by the way in which US companies were allowed to control parts of Chile as 'sovereign owners', 'where they impose their will despotically and their laws arbitrarily over workers and employees.'[13]

Allende was also indignant that the copper companies could make immense profits while Chile was forced to beg for loans, and he was outraged that nobody in the government appeared to know whether a copper agreement had been signed between the two governments, or even whether one had been signed with the copper companies. The confusion belied a cavalier attitude to Chile's main income and was an affront to Chile's national dignity. That the world copper market, and therefore Chile, depended on the whims of six US copper magnates made the situation a 'typical example of imperialism'.[14] Allende therefore pushed for the creation of a National Copper Corporation that would oversee copper production and that would sell Chilean produced copper on the world market so that the State would know what costs were involved and would be able to effectively control an important part of the economy.

Chile's experience in the Second World War was an example of this unjust situation. During the war the Roosevelt administration had fixed the price it would pay for copper (and other strategic materials) through the Metal Reserve while Chile agreed to sell its entire production to the United States. It cost Chile some US$500 million. 'Imagine, honourable colleagues, what could have been done with this extraordinary amount', Allende asked.[15] He also reminded the Senate that after the war, the value of Chile's currency reserves had fallen by 25 per cent thanks to the rise in the price of imports from the United States. This could not be allowed to happen again.

Thanks to Allende's work, a Department of Copper was created, which was able to buy copper from the US-owned copper companies and then sell it on the global market, diversifying Chile's export destinations. Although this was far short of the nationalisation that Allende sought, it was an improvement, albeit short-lived. With the end of the Korean War the United States released its copper stocks onto the world market, pushing the price down. Chile initially held onto its stocks to avoid pushing the price lower, but these stocks were then discovered to have been 'lent' to the US-owned Anaconda copper company, which promptly sold them on the world market. Prices fell further. Then in 1955 a new law was passed which gave the copper companies tax breaks and allowed them to take over the sale of copper again. When the Vietnam War began, the United States again forced Chile to sell its copper at just over half of its market value. Allende denounced the injustice but nevertheless, Chile, one of the world's poorer countries in effect subsidised the United States war effort by US$52 million.[16]

Allende was not just interested in copper's economic potential, but also in the fate of the people that worked in the industry. He noted that many workers contracted silicosis and that even as copper was being debated in the Senate, they were engaged in a strike in protest at the arbitrary treatment meted out by the copper companies. The strike had even involved US workers paid in dollars, who had subsequently been repatriated. If the welfare of the copper workers was poor, in the rest of the economy it was dire. As always, Allende demonstrated a deep concern for ordinary people and he worked hard to push through healthcare reforms that would benefit them. As a senator and the chairman of the Senate's Health Committee (1950–52), Allende was behind a law that regulated the working conditions of public doctors, as well as the bill on the creation of a National Health Service, which amalgamated Chile's existing healthcare bodies. These reforms much improved the working conditions of Chile's public doctors, and made the public health service more efficient. It was still not a comprehensive healthcare system, but it was a step in the right direction.

In 1954 Allende was elected vice president of the Senate. In June that year Guatemala's progressive government was overthrown and its President Jacobo Arbenz sent into exile, in an event that reverberated around Latin America. Allende protested the US intervention in his speeches. He condemned the Tenth Interamerican Conference that had been recently held in Caracas, as being designed to attack Guatemala under the pretext of attacking international communism. 'How is it possible that [the US] wants to fool us in front of the entire world, by calling the few democrats there are in the Caribbean 'Communists' while it considers the most abject governments and dictatorships that have flogged and subjugated their peoples with such unusual violence that they are the disrepute of America, democracies?' He also condemned the role of the United Fruit Company and its dramatic exploitation of Guatemala and other Central American countries, saying that it was 'indispensible to underline what the imperialist businesses are and how they "control" the political and economic life of peoples'. This control created dire poverty for the majority of Guatemalans. Guatemala's drama was that of a country that had 'rebelled in dignity in the search for a better destiny'. If in the future Chile was to take similar measures it too would 'surely feel over us the threat of foreign arrogance.'[17] For Allende, as for many Latin Americans, Guatemala was an outrage and a clear example of US imperialism.

Shortly afterwards Allende was invited to join a tour of the Soviet Union, which he joined with his wife despite strong criticism from within the Socialist Party. The Chilean delegation spent a month visiting the Soviet Union. Freed from the restrictions of public life in Chile, Allende felt relaxed and enjoyed himself. He was asked to write an article for Pravda, which was published in August 1954. He was excoriated in the Chilean press as an anti-patriot for having outlined Chile's economic reality to Pravda's readers – that 83 per cent of Chile's income came from the export of minerals and US companies took 88 per cent of the profits thanks to bilateral agreements, that Chile was forbidden from selling minerals to socialist countries, and that 87 per cent of the land was owned by less than 2,000 people.[18] While in the Soviet Union the Chileans decided to extend their visit to China. The group travelled onwards to Beijing, where they spent another three months. They attended the celebrations of the fifth anniversary of the Chinese Revolution and briefly met Mao Tse Tung and Chou En Lai. Allende therefore had the chance to experience something of the world's foremost socialist countries, and meet their leaders.

Following his return home Allende plunged himself back into his political work. The Ibañez government was failing to live up to people's expectations, and the economy was suffering from high inflation. Seeking ways to remedy the situation, on the initiative of the owners of the right-wing *El Mercurio* newspaper, the government invited a group of foreign economists to Chile. This team advocated wage freezes, reducing tariff barriers, cutting public spending and encouraging foreign investment – a precursor of the modern neoliberal programme. The measures succeeded in cutting inflation, but inflicted significant suffering on ordinary Chileans. The cuts also coincided with a fall in the price of copper. In April 1957 popular protests erupted and Santiago was rocked by mass rioting. The government declared a state of emergency, but it was the end of Ibañez's political life. The Popular Socialist Party abandoned his government, and in February 1956 it joined the People's Front. The new alliance was dubbed the Popular Action Front (FRAP) and shortly afterwards, in July 1957, the two Socialist parties reunited, recreating the Socialist Party of Chile. Two months later Salvador Allende was nominated the FRAP's Presidential candidate for the 1958 elections in a popular convention that included 2,000 delegates from social organisations across the country. Allende and the communists sought to further broaden the FRAP coalition. In 1957 the National Falange (who later became the Christian Democrats) and the Radical Party had allied with the left to overturn the proscription of the Communist Party, and Allende hoped the alliance could be extended into the presidential elections. However, there was significant opposition to this within the Socialist Party and the coalition remained 'working class'.

The 1958 FRAP campaign was full of hope and enthusiasm. The country seemed ready for change, the left was united and vibrant, and over the years people had become increasingly receptive to its message. The Communist Party was legal again, and new regulations made the voting process more transparent. And yet the campaign had no way of reaching its voters in the more isolated areas of the country. People often had to walk for hours to reach the nearest town. Salomon Corbalan, the Socialist Party General Secretary, had an idea. The campaign could use its links with the railway workers' trade union to hire and man a train to take Allende's message directly to the people.[19] At the time trains connected nearly the entire country and it would allow them to reach towns and villages that would have otherwise remained out of reach. The workers chose to use an old steam locomotive, painted it black and fixed the national coat of arms to the front. The destination was given as Santiago–Puerto Montt–La Moneda.[20]

Allende was accompanied by musicians, artists, intellectuals and political figures from the FRAP coalition. In a time before television, and when many Chileans did not even have radios, the arrival of the 'Train of Victory' was a real event, a chance to hear popular songs, poetry and to meet the stars of the day. The train stopped at 136 places on the route, up to ten stops a day. At each one, crowds of thousands gathered to listen to Allende.[21] In one village a peasant woman bent to kiss the hem of his trousers. Allende reacted angrily, lifting her to her feet. Back on the train, he sank his face into his hands and said, '*Compañeros*, I am not a messiah, and I don't want to be. I want to appear before my *pueblo*, before my people as a political option. I want to be like a bridge towards socialism.' However, for Allende, as for Monty Python's Brian, it was not for him to determine how many ordinary people saw him. But Allende foresaw a political problem if the people carried unrealistic expectations, 'We can't change this country in a matter of hours. And a woman that kisses trousers, or tries to kiss one's feet, is expecting miracles that I cannot provide, because the miracle has to be made by the people'.[22] Allende may not have liked it, but the peasant woman's action demonstrated that he had become a real symbol of hope for many ordinary people who thirsted for change. It was not the only old-fashioned gesture he received, many peasants asked Allende to be godfather to their children, and others, emulating peasant practice with their landlords, offered him their sisters or daughters. The contrast with the poorly attended meetings of 1952 was stark and confidence boomed through Allende's supporters. The X-shaped graffiti of a V superimposed over an A began to appear across Chile, its message simple and clear – Vote For Allende.

The optimism made for a relaxed campaign. A documentary maker filmed the campaign. For one clip the crew asked Allende to re-enact a speech he had given earlier that day, the recording would be added later. For the amusement of his collaborators he used the opportunity to swear and curse while making all the right expressions and gestures. The pre-recorded sound was added later, and nobody was the wiser until a letter was received from the director of a deaf school in Valparaiso complaining at the senator's market-stall language despite his 'being a doctor and coming from a good family'.[23]

Allende's companions on the 1958 campaign were astonished at their candidate's energy. Despite constant activity, speaking at least ten times a day and sleeping little, he never seemed to tire. Allende himself found his follower's amazement amusing. He could sleep like Napoleon, he explained, wherever he was, he could relax and sleep for five minutes and wake up fresh. Others recall him practising yogic breathing techniques to rest.[24] His collaborators also marvelled at his iron constitution, with Allende rarely succumbing to colds or other ailments. Allende himself used to jokingly recall a poem recited by another Socialist deputy to explain his energy: 'They say that the giant Antaeus used to embrace the ground to gather strength... I am no giant and no Antaeus... but I, as this mythical titan, embrace my people and from them I obtain the strength I need to struggle for you and for my *patria*.'[25]

Frightened by the gathering strength of Allende's campaign, his opponents tried to accuse him of demagoguery. As a provincial youth in metropolitan Santiago, Allende had cultivated a unique dress sense that had led to him being labelled a 'toff'. He also enjoyed good food, especially traditionally prepared seafood, and red wine. But Allende was far from being the frivolous snob that the media portrayed. In one attack the wealthy right-wing newspaper owners accused Allende of owning a yacht, something clearly beyond the reach of most Chileans. In response Allende organised for his sailing dinghy to be transported to Santiago, where he had it floated in a fountain on Bulnes Square. That afternoon a demonstration of 300,000 people assembled in the square to hear him speak, and he pointed out his floating 'yacht'. As with Allende's housing exhibition outside the Union Club in 1938, the evidence before people's eyes spoke more than a thousand words.

However, many people still distrusted politicians. Standing behind a thin wooden partition wall, Allende and Carlos Jorquera, one of Allende's collaborators and later press secretary overheard a conversation between two peasants after a stop on the 'Train of Victory'. One of the peasants doubted that Allende would fulfil his promises. After some debate the two made a deal. They would vote for Allende and work towards his victory, but if he betrayed them they would travel to Santiago and kill him 'so that nobody ever laughs at us peasants again.' Allende initially wanted to interrupt the two men, but thought the better of it. But he swore to Jorquera, 'these *compañeros* won't need to go to Santiago to kill me... you know why? Because I really will honour my word to them. I'd rather the right kills me for honouring my word to the peasants than that they consider me a traitor.'[26]

While the left was united around Allende's candidacy, the right united behind Jorge Alessandri. Two centrist candidates, Allende's friend Eduardo Frei, who stood for the newly formed Christian Democrats, and a Radical candidate were also in contention. A final candidate joined the fray in the last weeks of the campaign – Antonio Zamorano, the 'priest of Catapilco', whom many suspected of having his campaign financed by the right.[27] He would have a profound impact on the election results. The first two official counts gave Allende a narrow victory.

However, the news coming from the voting tables changed. While Allende was winning on the men's tables, the women were voting for Alessandri.[28] At 11.30 p.m. Allende headed home, where a small group of his comrades gathered to wait for the official result. The third official count also gave Allende victory, but some radio stations picked up on Alessandri winning on women's tables by a margin strong enough to give him victory. The Ministry of Interior, which usually kept the nation informed, maintained a strange silence.

The reason for the silence became clear at 1 a.m. when the doorbell rang at Allende's Providencia home. Ozren Agnic, Allende's congressional assistant, went to answer the door. Five senior military officers stood in the doorway. The officers explained that they had a personal message for Allende from the President, General Carlos Ibañez. Allende and Agnic listened as the officers told Allende that President Ibañez was holding back the final result to give Allende time to consider the offer of the Presidency 'in the interests of the nation' – in other words Ibañez was proposing to subvert the election result. Allende replied with contained anger, 'General, I have never heard such stupidity and monstrosity. I am extremely surprised that a General of the Republic should lend himself to be the messenger of this infamous manoeuvre.' 'Go back to where you came from and tell Mr Ibañez that I will be the first person to respect the verdict of the ballot boxes, as I will be the first to fight any seditious attempt in Chile.'[29]

When the results came in it became clear that Alessandri had won by a scant 33,000 votes. Zamorano received just over 41,000. Allende missed out on the Presidency by 3 per cent. With such a close margin Allende's relatively poorer showing amongst women had been key, and in a 1970 interview Allende wryly commented that in 1958 he had been 'defeated by the women'. In the same interview Allende indicated the contradiction that existed in his attitudes towards women. When asked about whether absolute equality between men and women was desirable, Allende answered 'a complete and absolute equality, with a complete and absolute difference', and in response to a question as to what kind of president Chilean women wanted

Allende responded 'clearly defined, virile, but at the same time, understanding, gentle and empathetic'. Then, in a subsequent question about which contemporary women he would like to dine with, Allende answered 'None. After dinner, with many. I'm discrete, I won't name names.' These answers perhaps indicate where Allende's weakness with women lay. Despite an attitude that recognised gender equality and the need for a distinct status for women, he understood women wanting a president as some kind of idealised partner, yet at the same time he was known for his womanising. Although this reputation probably won him some admiration among male voters it may well have alienated women across Chile who suffered emotionally and materially from men's infidelity. Yet womanising was a common feature of Chilean male society, and the extent to which it alienated women is hard to know. Furthermore, the politicisation of women's issues in Chile had not yet become a widespread phenomenon, and Allende was well known for pushing legislation that favoured women and children. It therefore seems as likely that Chile's very social structure affected Allende's ability to reach women voters. Women were far less likely to work outside the home, and their social networks were more likely to be dominated by the neighbourhood and the church. Allende consistently asked his supporters to convert their wives and girlfriends to the cause, but the issue of Allende's female vote was not resolved until the 1970 campaign when the Popular Unity began to organise community-based committees.

Many of Allende's supporters also suspected that the various forms of vote buying used by the right had also played their part, and some were willing to officially question the results. Allende remained firm and recognised Alessandri's victory. The 1958 campaign was a harsh defeat for the Chilean left, but paradoxically it was also a great victory. For the first time the left had been within touching distance of victory in a coalition of its own. The left's message had reached the entire country, and Allende was now a truly national figure – and the standard bearer of the left's unity.

5
Between Revolutions

Shortly after Allende's defeat in the 1958 elections, thousands of miles to the north, an anti-dictatorial rebellion matured into an outright revolution. On 1 January 1959 the Cuban Rebel Army entered Havana, overthrowing the Batista dictatorship. While initially the revolution's political direction was unclear, it soon became apparent that its leaders were aspiring to build socialism. The revolution and its growing conflict with the US inspired a generation of Latin Americans anxious for social change and brought the Cold War straight into 'America's backyard'. In the United States the revolution sparked fears that other countries might follow and it thus defined US policy towards Latin America for a generation. In Chile the revolution was to prove both an inspiration and a challenge for Allende and the left in general.

The Cuban revolution overshadowed Venezuela's return to democracy at the end of 1958 where elections brought Allende's old friend and Santiago neighbour, Romulo Betancourt, to power. Allende was invited to Betancourt's inauguration in Caracas alongside fellow Chilean politician Eduardo Frei. While in Venezuela, Allende decided to visit Cuba to see what was happening for himself. Allende's first impressions were not favourable. From his hotel window Allende saw the Miami and Havana police bands marching preceded by young women doing gymnastics. Allende was leaving the city when he bumped into Carlos Rafael Rodríguez, the leader of the Cuban Communist Party, who asked him what he was doing in Cuba. Allende told him 'I came to see the Revolution, but since there is no such revolution, I'm going.' Rodriquez told him not to be taken in by appearances and arranged for him to meet the revolution's leaders. Che Guevara soon sent a car and Allende met him in the eighteenth century La Cabaña fortress above Havana harbour. In a room lined with books, Guevara lay on a camp bed, inhaler in hand, recovering from an asthma attack. 'Come in *compañero*, you're a medic and you understand. Wait a minute and we can talk', he said.[1] They then had a discussion about the situation in Latin America, and the differences between the situations in Chile and Cuba.[2] Allende was then taken to meet Raul Castro, complete with plaited hair, who took him to see Fidel, who was presiding over a cabinet meeting. Allende was surprised by the informality of the set up. Fidel spoke standing up, 'there were peasants playing chess and cards, lying on the floor, machine guns and all' – a situation far removed from the parliamentary politics Allende was used to.[3] The two men had a discussion that laid the basis for a personal friendship that was to last until Allende's death. Castro wanted to know what Allende's position on the Communist Party was, and was satisfied to hear that he considered them his allies. They discussed the situation in Chile and the region and although Allende disagreed 'fundamentally and violently' with some of Cuban leader's positions, there was an overall understanding between them. A few months later, at the 26 July celebration of the revolution, Fidel Castro told Gloria Gaitan, who was standing alongside him 'I know the man that will make the next revolution in Latin America' before he introduced her to Allende.[4] Years later she travelled to Chile where she and Allende began a relationship, and she witnessed the last months of his government.

Allende returned to Chile shortly after this first visit to Cuba with his enthusiasm renewed. His early and direct contact with the revolution gave him a clear idea of where it was going, what the likely US response would be, and therefore, of what its impact would be upon Latin America and Chile. Later, when his own road to socialism began to be criticised as 'reformist', the contacts Allende had made in Cuba would be vital in shoring up his revolutionary credentials.

Following his return to Chile in late 1959, Allende set up the Popular Institute which was meant to act as a think tank for the left, and which managed to bring together a variety of left-wing social scientists to investigate Chile's social and

economic reality and provide data and proposals. The Institute
was the latest in a long line of efforts by Allende to systematise
the data available to him and the left in general, partly in order
to train left-wing social scientists in the real detail of national
problems and partly so as to provide the basis for future policies.
Allende also hoped that the Institute might serve to provide a
space for discussion and debate for left-wing activists in order
to foster a broader identity, and plant the seed of a FRAP
movement. Once more it was largely his own party that let him
down. The Socialists feared that the Communists would soon
take over any new organisation, funding for the Institute soon
dried up, and although it helped to train some specialists who
later served the Popular Unity, it was unable to foster a broader
left-wing identity.

Meanwhile, the radicalising effects of the Cuban revolution
reached Chile. Washington's efforts to 'contain' communism in
Latin America had a new urgency. In March 1960 Eisenhower
gave the nod to the development of an invasion force of Cuban
exiles, in an action reminiscent of the overthrow of Arbenz in
Guatemala. In May 1960 the Cubans established diplomatic
relations with the Soviet Union, and in August the United States
responded with the Declaration of San José, which obliquely
threatened Cuba. In April 1961 under Kennedy, US-backed exiles
invaded Cuba, and were defeated. Castro declared the revolution
to be socialist and nationalised US companies in Cuba. In Chile
the left was invigorated by the revolution, and membership of its
parties surged. The right responded with fear. The class struggle
evoked class solidarities across the region, and Allende once
again nailed his colours to the mast of the underdog.

In the Senate Allende declared the Cuban revolution to be
the next stage in Latin America's struggle for full sovereignty.
Revolutions in Mexico (1910) and Bolivia (1952) had shown
the way in their times, but the Cuban revolution was destined
to better them. He underlined the revolution's legitimacy while
highlighting that while the goals of the revolution in Chile
were similar, 'We have repeatedly expressed that, with differing
strategy and tactics, such a process ought to flower in the various
countries of Latin America, in order to end the stage of political

vassalage, economic exploitation, to end the anguish, the hunger and the misery of thousands...' In Cuba, Allende said he had witnessed a people spiritually and materially mobilised, and fully interpreted by their government. He underlined that he had seen nothing like this in Moscow, Beijing, or in the United States. He also condemned the media campaign demonising the revolution saying, 'it seems unnecessary to me to underline how UPI, AP and the information agencies controlled by North American capital have deformed and continue to deform what has happened in Cuba. This kind of information is only comparable to the kind that existed when that great international robbery was perpetrated years ago against Guatemala.'[5] Not only did this media campaign distort what was happening in Cuba, it also began to change the political environment in Chile and the rest of Latin America. Uncle Sam's baleful glare turned on the region, and nobody could escape its effects.

In 1960, three days after the Cubans celebrated the 26 July and announced the nationalisation of US companies on the island, Allende and other senators denounced an 'organised and planned' slanderous media campaign against them in a mayoral election in San Miguel. The aggressive tone of this campaign became characteristic. The FRAP leadership was accused of corruption and even murder. Allende responded with a harsh denunciation of the coordinated campaign by the media and government. The way victory was won foreshadowed the victory of the Popular Unity in 1970. In San Miguel communists had developed a 'popular university' which together with the hard work by FRAP councillors, had mobilised the population. However, the new timbre of the attacks against the left forced Allende's tone to change too. While he had never idealised Chile's democracy, he had always honoured it. Now, 'the unmeasured use of public power' in the service of an unworthy cause had further disfigured 'the putrefied channel of a democracy' that had already been warped by vote-buying.[6] While Allende always retained his faith in the possibility of a revolution that would overflow that 'putrefied channel', others would soon begin to question the wisdom of playing the democratic game. They would cause Allende more than one headache in future.

The first electoral campaign after the Cuban revolution took place in March 1961. To the horror of Allende's team of supporters, he accepted the PS Central Committee's nomination for the constituency of Valparaiso and Aconcagua. The Socialist vote was negligible in the region, and the other parties all had good candidates. However, Allende was thinking one step ahead. If he was able to win, his chances of being presidential candidate in the 1964 elections would be strengthened. This was not just optimism: the FRAP's showing on women's tables had much improved in the municipal elections, and in the 1958 presidential campaign he had developed a strong support base in the peasantry. If they worked hard enough, Allende was sure that they would be able to win over the peasants in Aconcagua. Over the objections of his team, Allende asked them to prepare a new campaign by convincing friends and collaborators to donate money, hold fundraising dinners or provide useful equipment.

Key to the success of the campaign was the 'Victory Bus', a large, if rickety, bus hired from an Allende supporter. A generator, a large canvas screen, a film projector and a sound system were mounted on it. Wherever the bus went it took a small team of painters and local singers and the bus was fitted with a portable stage on the roof. Inside it carried beds for the team, paints and printing materials. Like the 1958 train, it was a mobile campaign centre. The bus would be driven around a selected area, loudspeakers advertising the evening's event, then the bus would make a stop and the projector, screen, generator and stage would be set up. Short cartoons would be shown, followed by a longer political film. The crowd would be asked to bring newspapers that would then have Allende's image printed on them and the people would then paste them up in public places. Teams of painters would go out to paint rocks and walls with pro-Allende slogans. Often they would be arrested by police or beaten up by thugs hired by landowners – guards at one landowner's gates shot up the bus itself. The problem was particularly bad in rural areas. Peasants still lived in nineteenth-century conditions and were often illiterate. Laws were seldom applied and children rarely went to school. People lived without electricity or clean drinking water and subsisted in terrible poverty. Landowners even forced 'droit du seigneur' upon the daughters of their workers.[7] In such conditions it was not easy to exercise the right to a free vote. Despite these difficulties Allende's campaign was a great success and he won his senatorial seat, with enough votes for the two other FRAP candidates to get seats.[8] It amply demonstrated that Allende's appeal went beyond the parties of the left, and it was the miracle he needed to set himself up for 1964.

While Allende was winning yet another electoral battle, events in Latin America and the world were creating new difficulties for the left. The Cuban revolution and the guerrilla groups it inspired exacerbated fears of revolutionary change. Latin American elites welcomed US counter-revolutionary initiatives. Alongside a counter-revolutionary campaign against Cuba, the United States launched an economic and diplomatic offensive to isolate Cuba. Then in 1961 Kennedy proposed a set of economic, political and military measures to the rest of Latin America, an 'Alliance for Progress', to tackle the socio-economic roots of revolution by seeding economic growth. At the same time the United States moved to transform and extend training programmes for Latin American militaries. Intelligence agencies were set up or improved. The training was guided by a doctrine that emphasised an international communist threat through subversion, shifting the focus of Latin American militaries from external to internal threats. Soon the Latin Americans began to develop and adapt this doctrine, spawning a virulent right-wing ideology that built on earlier anti-communist and conservative ideas. When the promised economic growth failed to materialise the legacy of the Alliance was over-muscled and paranoid militaries with close links to the US defence establishment. It was no coincidence that country after country fell to right-wing dictatorships during the 1960s.

In Chile this process had a series of repercussions. The first was the beginning of direct and sustained US interference in Chilean politics, and the expansion of US military-ideological training for the military. The second was the radicalisation of some sectors of the Chilean left inspired by the Cuban revolution. Castro's Second Declaration of Havana in February 1962 was for many a call to arms: 'In many countries throughout Latin America, revolution is today inevitable. [...] what does the Cuban Revolution teach? That revolution is possible, that the people can make it, that in the contemporary world there are no forces capable of halting the peoples' liberation movement... The duty of every revolutionary is to make the revolution.'[9] To those who saw revolution as an armed triumph, this seemed to contradict the gradual, more evolutionary position of the traditional Chilean left embodied by Allende. The effects of the Cuban revolution were compounded by the Sino–Soviet split and Chinese accusations of Soviet capitulation to imperialism because of the policy of peaceful coexistence. The polarisation of politics challenged the traditional parties of the Latin American left from within, and in Chile resulted in the creation of an organisation that embodied the new revolutionary impatience, the Revolutionary Left Movement (MIR).

While a new challenge was gestating on the left, the forces behind Salvador Allende also faced a newcomer to their right. In 1957 the youth wing of the Conservative Party split, admitting the need for social change, and seeking to claim a space between the revolutionary left and a traditional right whose only response to calls for social justice was electoral fraud and repression. In 1958, now called the Christian Democrat Party (PDC), they put Allende's friend Eduardo Frei forward as presidential candidate. Frei, unflatteringly described by Pablo Neruda as a 'curious' and 'extremely calculating man' prone to 'parsimonious and frostily cordial' behaviour, was a tall aristocratic figure of Swiss descent, a conservative with a social conscience.[10] He was confident that he could emulate the success of European Christian Democracy. In 1958 Frei took nearly 21 per cent of the vote. It was an impressive debut, but in the wake of the Cuban Revolution, in the 1961 parliamentary elections PDC support fell to just over 15 per cent, showing how the radicalising effect of the Cuban revolution had benefitted the left. However, the PDC remained a national force, and it had one key advantage – support from European Christian Democrats, from the Catholic Church, and most importantly, from the United States.[11] It soon began to tell. By the 1963 municipal elections it was the largest single party in

Chile. The full-scale US intervention in Chilean politics after the Cuban revolution changed the political panorama and became one of Allende's and the left's main challenges during the decade.

In 1964 the FRAP had no realistic alternative candidate to Salvador Allende. His victory in Valparaiso and Aconcagua, his name recognition among the people, and their familiarity with his programme meant that there was no real debate this time. While the mechanics of the campaign followed a similar pattern to the previous two, with a 'Train of Victory' heading south, and a tour of the entire country, this campaign applied lessons learned in the past. Allende tried to remedy his weakness among women voters by setting up the CIMA (Independent Committee of Allendista Women) under the leadership of his then-Catholic and rather conservative sister, Laura. She would help to convince middle and upper class Chilean women that they had nothing to fear from Allende. An Allendista Catholic Movement was set up under Allende's old professor Cruz Coke to counteract the Christian Democrats. The campaign even counted on support from retired military officers in a Civic Military Front. Allende campaigned with his customary energy. It went well initially but Allende's campaign soon began to feel the effects of what the Church Committee later called 'a massive anti-communist propaganda campaign' funded by the CIA.

The propaganda campaign in the Chilean media aimed at demonising Allende and was complemented by US support for Allende's political opponents. It was a campaign that spared no expense, and broke the mould of previous Chilean elections, although the United States had been influencing media in Chile for years. The CIA station in Chile had begun supporting news wire services, right-wing intellectual magazines and a weekly newspaper in 1953. In 1961 the CIA established relationships with key political parties and created the mechanisms by which it would spread its propaganda. 'Electoral committees' were set up in Washington and Santiago to coordinate US efforts to subvert the democratic process in Chile. From 1962 to 1964 nearly US$4 million was spent on 15 'covert action projects'. The CIA involvement was such that it even covered over half the costs of the Christian Democrat campaign (over US$2.6

million) helping the PDC to run a US-style election campaign, supported by opinion polls, voting drives and so on.[12] The CIA also initially provided funding to the Radical Party. The CIA effort was complemented by US multinationals who also provided funds, in particular to the right-wing National Party.

While the material support for the PDC enabled it to win an outright majority in the 1964 elections, the propaganda campaign against Allende was judged to be more cost effective. This involved paying for street posters, leafleters, loudspeakers broadcasting from helicopters, graffiti painters, radio news slots, the cultivation of 'assets' in the Chilean media, notably in *El Mercurio*, as well as letter campaigns. 'Black propaganda' – false materials attributed to left-wing organisations, designed to promote arguments within the left – were also published. Many elements of the campaign sound primitive today, but they were effective enough. Radio programmes would be interrupted by machine gun fire, followed by screams as a woman shouted, 'The communists have killed my son!' followed by more machine gun fire. This propaganda dominated the airwaves across Chile, with dozens of broadcasts a day.[13] Allende protested against this campaign in the Senate, saying that the FRAP was being victimised in the same way as Balmaceda, Alessandri, the Popular Front and Ibañez had been victimised when they had tried to attack the privileges of the wealthy. He condemned this propaganda as dishonest because it did not focus on the concrete activity of any party, but on a 'disfigured image of communism' which was used to gain political advantage by creating a climate of panic and terror.[14]

The tipping point ironically came with a FRAP victory. In Curico a FRAP deputy died, forcing a by-election to take place. The right proposed an alliance to the Radical Party since their combined vote was 46 per cent and promised easy victory. The by-election became a rehearsal for the main event because Curico reproduced the national electorate on a smaller scale.[15] The FRAP put forward Oscar Naranjo, the son of the deceased, who surprised everyone by winning the election. Some within the FRAP were jubilant. Victory seemed assured. But Allende was not so sure. 'We'll see that the right, and everything that is behind it will not sit back now; they'll intensify the campaign against us, and I fear that we'll see important changes to the electoral picture over the next few days', he said to his collaborators. Salomon Corbalan was just as astute, 'We've won a deputy and lost a president', he said.[16] Defeat was sealed after the FRAP held a mass meeting of 300,000 supporters in Santiago. Allende knew the right would not fail to understand that to avoid him winning they would have to back Frei.

As Allende predicted, after the 'Naranjazo' victory in Curico, the CIA put its entire weight behind the Frei campaign, while continuing to fund the Radical Party candidate 'in order to enhance the Christian Democrat's image as a moderate progressive party being attacked from the right as well as the left.'[17] It wasn't all roses for the opposition to Allende. The increasing polarisation, and resistance to US interference forced a split in the Radical Party, and some of them declared their support for Allende. A Liberal party senator, protesting at US interference in the elections, also switched allegiances. However, the FRAP's victory had forced the opposition to unite and this did not bode well for Allende.

On election day Allende voted in Viña del Mar and then returned to Santiago. He had lunch with friends, and was unsurprised when the results began to give Frei the victory. He then walked over to his campaign offices, where before giving his loser's speech, he patted Osvaldo Puccio on the shoulder saying, 'don't worry, we'll win in 1970'. While those around him were devastated Allende remained optimistic. But the defeat was a heavy blow nonetheless. Allende resorted to humour, joking that on his gravestone it would read: 'Here lies Salvador Allende, future president of Chile.'[18] Some socialists took the defeat with less humour. One leader said that the PS would deny the new government 'bread and salt', but Allende, in an interview in Ercilla magazine on the day of Frei's inauguration, marked a different tone when he said, 'As a Chilean and as a man of the left I sincerely hope that Frei will be able to fulfil his promises to the people, but in the same way as he has a deep commitment to them, he also has tremendous commitments to the historic enemies of the people. Because of this his government will be an obstacle course and six years of contradictory pressures.'[19] Many ordinary socialists and communists were unable to take the defeat as philosophically. One communist recalled a comrade furiously exclaiming, 'And now what? How long are we going to continue with these elections?!'

If such opinions were becoming more commonplace among communists, among socialists, who had always had more serious problems with the 'electoral road' the effects were devastating. With many feeling that the electoral road was a chimera, a growing sector of the Party became more dogmatic in its understanding of revolution, edging away from the 'Allendista' vision, and towards a more 'orthodox' idea of the armed seizure of power. Stimulated by the appearance of guerrilla movements across much of Latin America, and by the influence of the Cuban revolution in particular, these socialists wanted to stop wasting time with elections, and start making the revolution.

Meanwhile Frei had won a victory large enough to govern without a coalition. In March 1965, again with US assistance, the PDC was able to win a majority in Congress. The Christian Democrats began to implement what they called the 'Revolution in Liberty', aggressively developing mass organisations, especially in unionising the countryside, and building the legislative framework for a large network of social organisations that went from neighbourhood organisations to women's organisations. These efforts brought large numbers of Chileans into the political process for the first time. Frei's 'Revolution in Liberty' promised much – an agrarian reform, banking reform, economic growth, and the 'Chileanisation' of the copper industry (buying majority stakes in the copper industry), but the question was whether it would be able to deliver without alienating its paymasters.[20]

Allende's words in Ercilla proved visionary. Frei and the PDC were unable to push through a large-scale agrarian reform against the vigorous resistance of the landed elites, their 'chileanisation' of the copper industry was a blatant injustice in a poor country with severe economic problems. The failure to resolve Chile's many structural problems despite high expectations led to increasing popular pressures. Strikes, demonstrations and land occupations took place increasingly, which the government responded to with repression. In April 1966 troops were called to put down a strike in the El Salvador mine, killing eight people. In 1967 a strike in Santiago led to the killings of several people. In 1969 police opened fire on shantytown dwellers in the city of Puerto Montt, killing ten people and wounding dozens. The government was unable to stabilise the economy, and inflation topped 30 per cent in 1967. Repression and economic instability encouraged more and more people to think of a more far-reaching process of change. Factions within the PDC moved leftwards, eventually splitting from the Party in early 1969, arguing for an anti-imperialist and socialist solution to Chile's problems.

A year after Frei was elected Allende made a harsh judgement of his government. Allende was embittered by the violence of the election campaign, which had viciously slandered his person as well as the movement he represented. Allende had always valued his friendships, and he always had friends from across the political spectrum but the 1964 election campaign had breached the limits of the 'most basic political and human consideration'. This was disloyal to their friendship and to Chile, because in Allende's eyes, by allowing the PDC to benefit from such a campaign Frei had put it at the service of US interests. 'It was a dirty victory.' Allende later said.[21] Allende therefore pulled no punches as he analysed the first year of Frei's government.

Allende denied that Frei's government was carrying out a revolution. According to him it was acting to prevent revolution by preserving capitalism, as had Christian Democrat governments in Italy and Germany. In the Chilean context this meant that the PDC had subordinated Chile's national interests to those of imperialism. As Allende said, 'the party that governs today has the strange privilege of having, at a crucial moment for Chile, silenced the yearning for self determination of our people through foreign pressure – foreign pressure both in inspiration and in the massive execution which distorted and confused national patriotic feeling.'[22] He accused the PDC of allowing Chile to become 'psychologically colonised'.

Allende became increasingly concerned with imperialism in the late 1960s since the PDC had taken on, nominally at least, many of the projects first proposed by the left, including agrarian reform, democratisation, educational reform, control of copper and other natural resources. Few now debated the need for these measures. The battleground had shifted to the purpose and manner of their execution. A focus on imperialism also allowed Allende to limit the growing attacks coming from more extreme groupings within the Socialist Party and outside it, which accused him of being a social democrat and not a 'true revolutionary'. The US interference in the Chilean political system through the 1960s made imperialism an economic and political reality for Chile, the left's main enemy along with the Chilean oligarchy, particularly since the decade saw a progressive weakening of the latter, which did not even field its own candidate in the 1964 elections.

Internationally, too, imperialism was an issue of massive importance. In 1964 the United States had supported, if not instigated, the overthrow of Joao Goulart in Brazil, and in 1965 US troops invaded Santo Domingo in the Caribbean. The US intervention in Vietnam escalated sharply the same year, deploying hundreds of thousands of troops and beginning a massive bombing campaign against North Vietnam. In response, in January 1966 the first Trilateral Conference was held in Havana, ostensibly to create a global alliance of revolutionary forces fighting imperialism. Allende was present. In a world full of national liberation movements waging war against colonialism Allende led a quiet and arguably unsuccessful left in Chile. However, he was elected leader of the Organisation of Latin American Solidarity (OLAS), the regional information section of the Tricontinental. In June 1966 Allende was back in Cuba participating in the founding of the OLAS, but this time, without the moderating influence of the Soviet Union, the tone was openly one of armed revolution. One participant recalled,

Among greetings, winks and backslapping the Cuban commanders came and went from the Hotel Havana Libre, mixing with the Latin Americans that dreamed of emulating them. Salvador Allende circulated solemnly, wearing a *guayabera* shirt. The pressure in favour of the armed struggle was immense. The hosts freely offered courses in guerrilla warfare. The talk was of FAL and M-1 rifles, and whoever didn't know the slang was called a 'softie'.[23]

Yet the reality of the various countries soon imposed itself. Each country's revolutionary process took its own path, often into obliteration. The OLAS never met again. The same year Allende was elected president of the Chilean Senate. Meanwhile Allende's association with the leading lights of armed struggle helped him to maintain his revolutionary credentials in the eyes of those Chileans who dreamed of an armed revolution.

A year later in Uruguay, Allende spoke at a meeting at Montevideo University in parallel to the second meeting of the Alliance for Progress being held in the same city. In this speech he condemned the Alliance for Progress as the latest machination of US domination, in particular for the way in which it had led to dictatorships across the region and pulled Latin America even further into debt. The region was now obliged to pay off the interest on the acquired debts, forcing it into an even more subordinate position with regard to the United States. For Allende, the solution to Latin America's problems had to be sought through integration, internally and through structural changes to the mechanisms of trade and the prices of Latin American exports. Allende condemned the new forms that US imperialism was taking in promoting regional integration through free trade, and establishing mixed ownership companies where Latin American governments held shares. These, Allende argued, did not alter US economic domination, and would not improve life for the mass of Latin Americans. US policies had, 'changed in their form, but not their content. The Big Stick was followed by Dollar Diplomacy. This was followed by the Good Neighbour Policy, and now the Johnson Doctrine. Always domination and arbitrary domination.'[24] The only solution for Latin America was to achieve economic independence, without which there could be no political independence.

A few months later, Che Guevara was killed in Bolivia. The survivors of his guerrilla column desperately sought to escape. In Chile some socialists, including Allende's daughter Beatriz, had previously set up a support network known as the ELN

(National Liberation Army). The news of Che's death was a
political earthquake for the left. Allende recalled his meetings with
Guevara in a heartfelt homage in the Senate, where he showed
his signed copy of Che's 'Guerrilla Warfare' where Guevara
had written 'To Salvador Allende, who seeks the same ends by
different means.' Yet even here Allende reminded his audience
inside and outside the Senate that Guevara had not blindly
supported the armed struggle. Allende showed that Guevara
had written that armed struggle could only take place where
civic competition was no longer possible, reminding everyone
that in Chile the popular movement had in fact nearly reached
power through these means.[25] Yet not everyone understood or
believed the message. Just over a month later the Socialist Party
held a Congress in Chillan. Che's example motivated a series of
resounding resolutions declaring the inevitability of the violent
seizure of power. Allende was booed off stage ('They didn't let
me speak! And on top of that they whistled me off! My own
comrades!' he said), and the Congress once again refused to
select him for the Central Committee.[26] The Chillan resolutions
were taken by the media to demonstrate the 'true' nature of
the Socialist Party, when in reality they were an expression of
frustration with the democratic road, as well as an emotional
homage to Guevara.

With the news that the survivors of Che's guerrilla column
were heading to Chile, the Chilean ELN, and the left as a whole,
mobilised to receive them. At the same time the government
mobilised the security forces to find the guerrillas as soon as
possible. Allende, with his usual political nous, knew that their
arrival in Chile was a hot potato for the Frei government. It
could not be seen to be handing revolutionaries over to their
executioners, and nor could it be seen to be supporting them.
As a senator, Allende was able to communicate with the
government, the Cuban authorities and with the Chilean left,
Allende suggested that the guerrillas be provided temporary
political refuge, before being flown to Easter Island, and then
onwards to Tahiti, where French authorities would guarantee
their onward travel to Cuba. Allende accompanied them. The
Chilean media had a field day. Allende was accused of being a

'guerrilla senator', and of having abused his position as President of the Senate. He was also subjected to a campaign of lies and sarcasm, which did its best to portray him as a buffoon, a man desperate for attention and in the pay of Cuba.[27] It seemed, as Miguel Labarca commented, as if his image was at the point of being destroyed.[28]

When Allende was cornered he came out fighting. This time he challenged the editors of Chile's main newspapers to a debate to be broadcast on television and radio. For over four hours Allende took apart his opponents. He reminded the listeners that the editor of *El Mercurio* had been a member of the Chilean Nazi's. The editor of *La Segunda*, a former leftist from Valparaiso, was left looking like an avaricious traitor who had betrayed his former comrades for money. The editor of *La Nacion* – the government newspaper – was reminded that in the nineteenth century his own grandfather had sought to create an army of Latin Americans to liberate Cuba from Spanish colonialism. How could such people criticise Allende's behaviour? Allende's opponents were left floundering and his popularity rocketed.

In a second part of his defence Allende took to the floor of the Senate. Here he explained why his actions had been legal, and explained why international solidarity was vital to 'social fighters under assault across Latin America.' In this speech Allende defended his life's work in parliament and his reputation. Over the years, he said, 'everything has been said of me, except that I am dishonest', Allende continued 'for me politics is about principles, about convictions. I have been honourable in my public life and my hands are free of blood and embezzlement.' As a man with an old fashioned sense of honour, Allende could tolerate attacks that targeted his politics, but not those against his reputation.

Allende protested that the media campaign against him had been 'planned, organised and measured', and that having failed to undermine the popular movement in successive elections, the campaign had moved to target Allende himself, making him the victim of 'jibes, ridicule, grotesque caricature, and anonymous sneers'. He reminded the Senate of his long career, that he had been the first to seriously talk about the need for agrarian reform, the first to call for the nationalisation of copper, and to call for fairer taxation, the very measures that many of them now supported. If he was ambitious, he said, it was because the presidency was 'a means to make real what one feels, believes and desires, to put in play one's convictions and doctrines.' Finally he reminded the Senate that he had suffered for his political opinions, having been expelled from university, imprisoned and blacklisted. He and his family had also suffered 'many very bitter hours' thanks to attacks the kind of which 'I do not wish for any of you', he said. It was dishonourable that he be accused of being an unsubstantial man without principles, when, as he reminded them, his hands had also carried out 1,500 autopsies and he had earned his bread 'sticking them in pus, cancers and death.'

Allende then refuted the accusation that he supported violence, repeating that guerrilla movements 'will spring up wherever implacable dictatorships impede the right of men to participate even in bourgeois democracy'. He defended the Cuban and Bolivian guerrillas as 'soldiers of Latin American independence' and underlined that since they shared a vision of a socialist Latin America without imperialism they were the brothers of the Chilean left. The Chilean popular movement had a duty to support those who fought for the Latin American revolution whether legally or with weapons. Imperialism was a key issue, and he reminded his audience that Chile could not be independent while its copper, nitrates, iron and other fundamental riches were under foreign control and while imperialism 'strangles our destiny.'[29] With this daring defence Allende was able to turn imminent defeat into victory.

Although he had saved his reputation and therefore his ability to stand as a presidential candidate in the upcoming 1970 elections, Allende clearly needed to broaden the electoral coalition that had so far failed to get him into power in 1958 and 1964. The lesson of these failures was clear to anyone willing to look back to the only time that the left had been part of government – the Popular Front. Back then the Radical Party had been the leading political force of the coalition, limiting the scope for change. This time the situation was different. Firstly, the communist and socialist parties were both well-entrenched, national forces. The union movement was strong and united. Furthermore, in the 1964 and 1965 elections the Radical Party had been barged off the centre ground by a vigorous and foreign-supported Christian Democrat party. In power the PDC had ruled alone and had failed to deal with Chile's structural problems. For the radicals, the left held out the possibility of a return to power as part of a broad coalition, albeit this time as a junior partner. Left-leaning radicals won the argument. The problem was, would the socialists accept them? After Chillan, the Socialist Party had seemingly rejected any possibility of an electoral alliance which included non-Marxist parties. However, this did not deter Allende from trying to build one anyway. The first signs that such an alliance was possible came in the Cautín by-election in 1968. Here, socialists and communists successfully voted for a radical candidate, but the future alliance still lacked a declared leader.

By the late 1960s there were voices calling for a fresh face to lead the left. Once more Allende had to stake out his right to stand. The parliamentary elections of March 1969 would make or break his chances. Allende switched constituency, asking to be candidate for the Magallanes region of the south that he had represented in 1945. He had two reasons for doing so. In late 1967 a fraction of the PS under Raul Ampuero split from the party. Ampuero was senator for the south, and he controlled the PS apparatus in the region. It looked like he was in an unassailable position. The loss of this seat, and the survival of a socialist faction there, was dangerous for the Party, and for the hopes of the left as a whole. Allende knew that if he was able to teach Ampuero a lesson and regain the South for the PS he would be doing the party a favour, as well as decisively demonstrating his popularity, as he had done in Valparaiso in 1961. Allende deployed his traditional methods, speeches, meetings, dinners, travelling to the places where ordinary people lived and worked. Thanks to his extraordinary memory he could recall the names of places and events from 20 years earlier, and he was able to roundly defeat Ampuero, destroying his faction and rebuilding the PS networks in the region. The victory, as he had expected, underlined his status as the man to turn to when an important victory was required.

The parliamentary elections also paved the way for the nomination of a left-wing candidate for the 1970 elections. Having demonstrated the strength of his candidacy Allende decided to leave Chile for a while in order to escape the inevitable debates and discussions. According to Miguel Labarca he knew that events demanded the creation of a broad alliance, and he was convinced that he was the only viable candidate to lead such a coalition. This was characteristic of his political nous and his self-confidence. Allende would joke that he was like Coca-Cola – a product well known in the market. But it was not just that he was well known, it was also that he truly believed he was the left's best candidate.

In the meantime Allende set out for a tour of North Korea, Vietnam and Cuba. He was inspired by the dignity the people of these countries showed in the face of adversity and he admired many of the advances they had made in education and healthcare. Allende later said his belief in socialism had been strengthened by witnessing how in the wake of tremendous destruction, North Korea had created a universal education system. He saw factories, and villages that 'have all the services that our urban population lacks: polyclinics, schools, chemists, small hospitals, nurseries and a normal level of nutrition for children'. In Vietnam he admired the courage of a people facing massive aerial bombardment. Allende was taken to see a jungle university that had 35,000 students, as well as hospitals where the wards were made of bamboo, and where every bed had a bomb shelter dug out next to it. Allende was deeply moved by his meeting with the Vietnamese leader Ho Chi Minh. He later recalled how Ho Chi Minh addressed his visitors in the Spanish he had learned as a kitchen hand on an Argentinean ship, thanking them for coming so far to show their solidarity with the Vietnamese people. These visits, in particular the visit to Vietnam had a profound impact on Allende. Allende imagined what Chile could achieve under socialism if it had the chance – 'from afar, with Chilean feelings and passion, I looked on and thought of our copper, the iron, nitrates, I thought of the forests, of our sea, that emporium of the greatest riches, and I thought too of our own people, who are also heroic and selfless.'[30] Witnessing the destruction of Korea and Vietnam must have made him think of what imperialism would do to prevent Chile achieving socialism.

Despite Allende's conviction and his recent victory in Magallanes, he was by no means a certainty as presidential candidate for 1970. For many in the political parties it was time for a new face for the left. They doubted that Allende could attract radicalised youth and he had never polled very well with women. At the same time the Communists had made it clear that they would not back a narrow coalition as in the past. If they were going to lose they preferred to do so with their own candidate.[31] Each party put forward a candidate. The Communists symbolically put forward Pablo Neruda, but they were mostly concerned with achieving a consensus around the future candidate. The Radicals favoured their own leader Alberto Baltra. Meanwhile within the Socialist Party leadership there were those who wanted a new face to lead them, and those who thought of the upcoming election as a symbolic gesture. These groups pushed the candidacy of Aniceto Rodríguez, the Party's General Secretary, planning to launch his campaign and create a fait accompli while Allende was away. However, on the eve of the proclamation Allende sent an urgent message from Cuba renouncing his candidacy and saying it was time to put the party before 'any egocentric attitude'.[32] At a stroke Allende had prevented the imposition of a candidate by the party leadership, and the stage was set for an open discussion.

Nobody in the Socialist Party wanted to trigger the race, so the Deputy General Secretary proposed that the Central Committee consult with the Regional Committees of the Party to see who they backed. They found that all but one supported Allende. However, Allende had few backers in the Central Committee, and it held back. On 26 August its members were called to vote on the matter. In the hall, as one participant later recalled, the atmosphere was 'anything but fraternal.'[33] No written record of the vote exists, and testimony of the vote is contradictory. What all accounts agree on is that Allende won largely because many Central Committee members abstained.[34] As Luis Corvalan, the

leader of the Communist Party, later said, Allende's nomination
as the PS candidate was a 'forceps birth.'[35] It was through the
resounding backing of the grassroots that Allende went forward
as Socialist Party candidate to lead the new coalition.

On 9 October 1969, after months of meetings and informal
conversations the Popular Unity (Unidad Popular, UP) coalition
was declared. The new coalition consisted of the Radical Party,
the MAPU (which had split from the Christian Democrats in
May 1969), and a small party called the API (Independent
Progressive Alliance) as well as the old parties of the FRAP.
The coalition agreed a political programme by December, but
was unable to agree on a leader. The UP set the New Year as a
deadline to decide but the date came and went. According to
Luis Corvalan the situation was sometimes 'tense and on the
verge of explosion.'[36] Although they had hoped for a negotiated
consensus the Communists finally decided to openly back
Allende, and the smaller parties were persuaded to withdraw
their candidates.[37] Allende would lead the UP into the elections.

The creation of the Popular Unity was the culmination of a
30-year effort by Allende and his Communist allies to create a
broad alliance of all possible social sectors around a programme
designed to put Chile on the road towards socialism. It was
the 1970 re-creation of the 1937 Popular Front, only this time
the alliance was clearly dominated by Marxist parties and
structural change was on the agenda. It was achieved despite
the opposition of the Chilean elite and US interventionism, and
in the face of the increasing dogmatism of some sectors of the
Chilean left. It was achieved in large measure thanks to Allende's
tireless campaigning over many years, which aimed at appealing
to 'a million consciences' rather than just getting votes, and
thanks to the efforts of those Communist and Socialists who
had long backed the idea of a broader alliance of the left and
the centre.[38]

Despite his good physical condition Allende paid a price for
the intensity of his work, and the pressures of campaigning.
In the run up to the election he suffered a minor heart attack,

which was kept secret. For two weeks Allende was treated at home while his intimate circle staved off rumours. His closest collaborators, and his daughter Beatriz, who was also a doctor, decided that the best treatment was for Allende to keep working. They did, however, prescribe a glass of whisky before bed. Allende returned to the campaign trail.

6

The Popular Unity

On 4 September 1970, Salvador Allende won the Chilean presidential elections. As was usual in Chilean elections nobody had won an overall majority (1964 had been an exception) and Congress was called to ratify the election result. Allende had polled 36.6 per cent, Jorge Alessandri, the right-wing candidate 34.9 per cent, and the Christian Democrats under Radimiro Tomic, 27.8 per cent. The results hid clear support for a socialist programme, with the PDC espousing what it called 'communitarian socialism', and showed how the left had gained from disillusion with the PDC, whose popularity had suffered after six years of government, a sorry economic record and a catalogue of massacres. The PDC had also been abandoned by its foreign backers, who had observed how the left had come to dominate the Party. In June 1969 some in the PDC had even sought to make an alliance with the UP official policy. The debate was fierce, and the motion was narrowly lost, leading to a split in the Party.[1] The grassroots of the Christian Democrats chose to put forward Radimiro Tomic, a left-leaning candidate who led the wing of the party opposed to Frei. The right-wing leadership of the PDC had lost control. With the failure of the CIA's programmes to develop a non-Marxist popular base and to divide the union movement, the CIA decided not to support a particular candidate and to concentrate on attacking the Popular Unity, the tactic from the 1960s that it judged to have been most successful.[2] In all, the CIA spent between US$800,000 and US$1,000,000 on the 'spoiling campaign' in 1970, with US transnational corporations also contributing funds.[3] The campaign evoked fears of a red terror, with images of blindfolded prisoners before a firing squad and Soviet tanks in central Santiago, radio programmes, and other stories planted in the media. Although the campaign failed to prevent Allende's victory, it contributed to further polarisation and to a financial panic. Despite this the results showed that nearly 65 per cent of the electorate had backed programmes that espoused some form of socialism.

On the day of the election Allende went to the Socialist Party HQ and then accompanied Tencha to vote. On arrival at the polling station they were met with applause mixed with whistles and jeers. The couple then returned to their home on Guardia Vieja street where they waited with friends and comrades.[4] As usual each party prepared its victory celebrations just in case but had to get final permission from the army, which provided security during the elections. Allende called the officer in charge to get permission for a UP celebration. The officer informed him that it had been approved. Allende put down the phone and said, 'We've won!' If not, permission would have been denied. The people assembled in his dining room erupted into cheers and hugs of joy. At 1 a.m. Allende walked to the nearby FECH building. The people of Santiago had begun gathering on Alameda Avenue, bouncing up and down in unison chanting 'If you don't jump you're a *momio*!'[5] Throughout Chile thousands of people celebrated victory, among them many Christian Democrat supporters. Allende thanked the people and the popular parties for a clean victory, reminding them that Chile's was a different kind of revolution which, 'does not mean destroying, but building; it doesn't involve demolishing, it involves constructing'. He finally underlined that the Popular Unity were the legitimate heirs of the founders of the nation, and that together 'we will make the second independence, the economic independence of Chile'.[6] Now, although its first victory had formally been won, the real battle was just beginning.

Allende and the Chilean popular movement faced many powerful enemies both in Chile and abroad, and their influence began to be felt immediately. It was an extremely tense situation. Although Allende's victory was promptly recognised by the Christian Democrat candidate, Radimiro Tomic, and celebrated by many of the Party's supporters, the leader of the Party and former President of Chile, Eduardo Frei, refused to do so. The

Figure 6.1 Salvador Allende with a group of workers from the Sumar textiles factory in Santiago.

situation was further complicated because the CIA was heavily involved in trying to prevent Allende's accession, using the now notorious 'Track I and Track II' options. Track I involved trying to get Frei re-elected by having Congress choose Alessandri over Allende, with Alessandri then resigning, opening the way for a 'special election' in which Frei would be the candidate. However, it rapidly came to involve seeking Frei to instigate the military option. Track II, meanwhile, rested on identifying officers willing to lead a military coup directly.[7]

Three days after the election, on 7 September, Allende went to see Frei in the Moneda palace. Allende knew that a cold distance had grown between himself and his former friend, but he tried to relax the situation. After greeting each other Allende ran to the presidential chair and sat in it. 'How do I look?' he joked. Seeing Frei was unamused he tried to cheer his old friend up. 'Don't worry *flaco* [slim], I'll give it back to you in '76.'[8] Although Frei was not up to joking, he reassured Allende that he was setting up a transition team. He lied. On the day that Allende took over the presidency the Moneda palace was completely empty. Frei's team did not even leave the internal phone directory.[9] Despite the initial rebuff, Allende continued to try to build a relationship with Frei, and asked for a mutual friend, Gabriel Valdes, Frei's former Foreign Minister, to arrange another meeting at which it became clear that Frei would not support Allende. According to Altamirano, Allende said Frei greeted him coldly, saying, 'What have you done? This entire thing of yours will fail!'[10] Embittered by electoral defeat, and jealous that Allende might succeed where he had failed, Frei warned that he could never support a government that contained communists.[11] At the same time Frei was now under pressure from the CIA to mount a coup against himself by appointing a military cabinet before the handover, and was being informed of US intransigence and hostility if Allende were to assume power.[12] He also knew of plans afoot to mount a coup. Meanwhile, Frei remained silent in public. With the outgoing government unclear on its position with regard to Allende, attention inevitably drifted towards the armed forces. Their position would be decisive in resolving the situation.

The armed forces were commanded by General Rene Schneider, a strict constitutionalist who had been appointed by Frei to impose obedience to the law after the 1969 'Tacnazo' mutiny. Schneider's position, along with that of the parties of the UP, had remained immovable during those vital days: the army should be apolitical and subordinated to civilian authority. In 1970, thanks to this position, the onus returned to the politicians in Congress and a coup was avoided.

Within the PDC, popular pressure, and fears of what the left's supporters might do if blocked from taking power, forced the right wing of the party to accept Allende's victory. At the same time they predicated their approval of Allende upon the signing of a pact of constitutional guarantees that they felt would guarantee the rule of law and pluralism in Chile. Allende signed the guarantees on 15 October. The deal allowed Allende to take power, effectively as the president of the 65 per cent of Chileans that had voted for broadly similar programmes of change.

The only option left for Allende's opponents was now a military coup. The more extreme Chilean opposition found a ready ally in the United States, and President Nixon ordered the CIA to begin preparations for Track II – a military coup in Chile (and possibly the assassination of Allende). Plans to destabilise the Chilean economy were drawn up as part of plans to create the psychological climate for a coup. While the CIA coordinated these plans, terrorist violence struck Chile for the first time. Bombs targeted supermarkets, the stock exchange, a television channel, railway lines and the main airport's fuel depot. Although the media attributed many of the attacks to mysterious and previously unknown left-wing groups, it was clear that the real instigators were right-wing groups opposed to an Allende government, which were being funded by the CIA.[13] On 22 October things went even further: a group of assailants, with whom the CIA was covertly involved, tried to kidnap General Rene Schneider two days before Allende was due to be confirmed. He was shot and died the next day. Schneider's killing showed the desperation of the right, and it sparked outrage and shock, ensuring that Congress voted Allende in.

Allende and his team knew that he was next on the list. He told one Christian Democrat friend that he had been shot at while getting out of his car some days earlier.[14] During the whole period prior to his confirmation Allende had been forced to sleep at different houses every night for fear of assassination. After 4 September, a group of MIR members provided his security. Although the MIR leadership had no confidence in Allende's victory they had proposed the arrangement some weeks earlier. For Allende, it was an effort to integrate the MIR into the process, while influencing its leadership. For the MIR it was a way of gaining access to privileged information, and to weapons and training. The two motives contradicted each other, and eventually led to the MIR being expelled from the protection detail in mid 1971.[15] The MIR's presence around Allende also confused his political opponents. After all if Allende was a democrat why were people who called for violent revolution protecting him? During talks prior to Allende's assumption of power Frei repeatedly asked Allende to dissolve the GAP, since they were extremists and it was not correct that they protect the life of the President of Chile.[16] Whether or not this was the real motive, Allende could still not rely on the police to be completely loyal, nor did they have experience in protection since Chile had no history of assassinations. The regular contacts with the MIR led to exchanges of information between it and the UP leadership, particularly in regard to seditious activity in the military, but it was an uneasy relationship that was testament to Allende's efforts to try to bring together the broadest possible spectrum of support for his revolutionary project.

With Allende confirmed, the transfer of power took place on 4 November. Eduardo Frei arrived riding in a horse and carriage and surrounded by plumed cavalry. He wore the traditional top hat and tails. Allende wanted to show that he would be a different kind of president. Throughout his life Allende had operated within the system, but meticulously not of it. In 1937 when he was elected to Congress he had asked the President of Congress to allow the Socialist deputies to take their oath the day after the others, and when Queen Elizabeth had visited Chile in 1967, as President of the Senate he had asked if he could forego the customary morning suit, and wear a well tailored dark suit instead. On his inauguration Allende did the same. He arrived by car wearing a dark suit, and afterwards he walked from the Congress to the cathedral through cheering crowds alongside his newly sworn-in cabinet ministers.[17]

Allende's inauguration marked the failure of US efforts to prevent a Marxist government from coming to power in Chile. Two days later, on 6 November, President Nixon convened the National Security Council (NSC) to discuss ways of bringing Allende's government down. For Nixon, Allende's effect on Latin America was dangerous. 'If we let the potential leaders in South America think they can move like Chile and have it both ways, we will be in trouble', 'Latin America is not gone' he continued, 'and we want to keep it.'[18] Following this meeting the decision was taken to maintain an outwardly 'cool and correct' position, but at the same time to undertake 'vigorous efforts' to ensure that the rest of Latin America understood their opposition, as well as seeking their cooperation against Chile, while blocking all forms of external economic and financial cooperation with Chile.[19] On 25 November Kissinger outlined five main points to the Covert Action Program [sic] to be undertaken against Allende's government: political action to divide and weaken the Allende coalition, extending contacts in the Chilean military, provide support to non-Marxist political groups and parties, assisting opposition media outlets and using them to 'play up Allende's subversion of the democratic process and involvement by Cuba and the Soviet Union in Chile.'[20] This programme of interference set the scene for Allende's entire time as President, providing his opposition with undreamed of resources, creating instability, undermining negotiations, exacerbating economic problems and encouraging the violent subversion of the Popular Unity process.

However, at first the opposition was too divided and demoralised to be able to prevent the Popular Unity from starting to implement its programme. This programme proposed 40 specific measures to deal with Chile's 'profound crisis'. It envisioned the expansion of democracy and the transformation of existing institutions in order to 'open the way for the most democratic government in the history of the country.'[21] It was, in essence, a summary of the measures proposed in Allende's previous campaigns. As Allende wanted, and as was most practical, the coalition left the details to be worked out later, during discussions between the political parties and the new mechanisms of popular power outlined in the programme.

The programme called for a new constitution and a single chamber parliament, and for simultaneous local, regional and national elections.[22] It proposed allowing the recall of public officials and politicians. Workers and social organisations would be given a role in power, helping to analyse and resolve problems. The judiciary would be reformed in order to favour the poor. In defence a new vision of sovereignty would place the Chilean people at its centre. The armed forces would be better-funded and integrated into society and the economy. A series of social reforms were projected – equal pay for men and women, the provision of a living wage for all, to extend social security, and a guarantee of 'preventative and curative' medical care to all. A vast new housing programme was planned, built by private and mixed firms. The programme also guaranteed equal legal status for women, and 'illegitimate' children.[23] In education a national state school system was planned, and a literacy drive would aim to end adult illiteracy. Sport would become a central part of education, and a new 'popular culture' would be promoted in society at large.

A central aspect of the programme was to be the reform of the economy into three related sectors, the social sector, the mixed sector and the private sector, linked by a process of democratically decided planning. The most important step would be the nationalisation of the copper, nitrates, iodine, iron and coal industries, the banking system, foreign trade (to prevent the export of vital goods for private gain), and of the country's largest monopolies. The Popular Unity also committed itself to finishing the land reforms begun under Alessandri and Frei.[24] The UP's land reform programme envisioned the creation of cooperatives and state-owned farms, as well as giving land titles to individual peasants. The programme also provided for the restitution of lands and the provision of resources to Chile's indigenous communities. In foreign relations the Popular Unity would condemn all forms of colonialism and neo-colonialism, and revise or cancel all pacts and treaties that Chile had signed with the United States. The programme in effect condensed 40 years of left-wing aspirations.

Although many of these measures may not seem particularly radical to Europeans accustomed to the existence of a welfare state, there were several important differences. In Chile the provision of welfare was to be linked in to a transformation in the way people acted and thought of themselves. They were not to be passive recipients of state largesse, but active participants in a process that provided the means for a dignified life, and in return demanded their participation in the management of the welfare system. Participation was to be demanded at every level. Workers were to participate in management of enterprises, and trade unions and other social organisations were to be incorporated into administering enterprises, and in the planning process. The government's first act in power was to sign an agreement legally recognising the CUT trade union federation for the first time since its establishment nearly 20 years earlier. The deal had previously been debated in trade union assemblies, and was the first step towards workers' incorporation into power under Allende.[25]

Figure 6.2   Salvador Allende speaking during the CUT anniversary, Santiago, 1 May 1971.

The hope was that the people could be incorporated into every aspect of decision-making, in a process of democratisation that went beyond the realm of elections and made the exercise of power a daily reality. This would not only change the way

Chile worked, it would change the way people behaved. It was the Chilean method of creating the revolutionary 'new man'. In practice the government tried to channel and subordinate these organisations to the grand strategy being followed by Allende. As the situation polarised towards the end of 1972, the structures of this 'revolution from above' came into conflict with alternative ideas and structures developed autonomously outside the UP.

The Popular Unity's foreign policy was also revolutionary in that it proposed a sea change in Chile's relations with the rest of the world. Chile would no longer accept a subordinate place within an international system dominated by the United States, and would no longer accept the primacy of foreign interests. By doing so it would help to 'liberate the powerful countries [currently] condemned to exercise despotism.'[26] This emphasis on sovereignty and participation precluded Chile's acting in the interests of any foreign power, and taken as part of a plan to put Chile on the road to socialism, was a revolutionary proposal.

The first seven of the government's '40 measures' proposed limiting the pay of top public servants, ending the use of external advisers, depoliticising bureaucratic appointments, stopping the private use of government vehicles, and ending expensive jaunts abroad. The Popular Unity promised to provide pensions to anyone over 60 who hadn't been able to pay enough contributions to retire, and to include small and medium businesses into the social security system. A ministry of family protection would be created, and free milk and breakfast would be provided to all children. Mother and child clinics and legal advice centres would be created in every neighbourhood, and every neighbourhood would be provided with electricity and clean water. Rents would be fixed at 10 per cent of family income and no more.[27] Many of these measures would still be relevant to Chile today.

The Popular Unity government carried with it a tremendous weight of expectation, but its unity was fragile. While the parties of the UP had united around a path to power, the purpose of holding that power was still a divisive issue. For some, including Allende himself, holding the presidency was a way of beginning a process of changes that would lead to the consolidation of socialism by means of gradual measures that would transform the basis of the economy, political system and the institutions of the state. 'Our country, starting from its traditions, will use and create the mechanisms that, within a pluralism based on the great majorities, will make possible the radical transformation of our political system', Allende said.[28] The country's existing institutions might serve foreign and elite interests, but the UP sought to transform their use gradually and from within, discarding or replacing only what was necessary. The great advantage of this approach was that it built on existing foundations, saving time, resources, and most importantly – lives.

For others within the UP the purpose of taking the presidency was to open the way to smashing the old institutions in order to replace them with new ones. Since the old institutions had served the bourgeoisie and the interests of US imperialism they could not be transformed. This meant creating parallel institutions that would overcome existing ones. This focus made the role of the military and the existence of a popular alternative 'own force' an important aspect of policy. This more 'traditional' vision of the revolution increasingly entered into conflict with Allende's. This problem was exacerbated by the fact that both Allende and the Communist Party justified their vision using the traditional framework.[29] The Popular Unity was a new method to achieve the same goal as the traditional revolution – socialism.

How this socialism was defined depended on who was talking. For Allende pluralism, free speech and individual liberty were a key part of socialism, but many others within the Popular Unity had not given much thought to whether the UP would be a stage on the road to Soviet-style socialism, or whether it would be the beginning of a new version. Many no doubt thought that such issues could be worked out along the way in the interplay of discussions within the left.

Although this approach was practical in that it minimised the scope for disagreement within the UP, it also made it difficult for the Popular Unity to make allies beyond the left. If traditional socialism was the goal, what would happen to the bourgeoisie? The non-Marxist parties were presumed to pass into opposition at some point further down the road, and the Communist leader

Luis Corvalan invented a metaphor for this, stating that the Popular Unity was like a train travelling from Santiago to Puerto Montt – passengers would get off at stops before the final destination. The problem was, what would happen to them once they did?

The two perspectives on the nature of the revolution demanded different approaches to the issue of power. For those wanting to smash the 'ancien regime', the development of class-based unity and of alternative 'popular' institutions that could challenge those of the state were essential. They believed that violent conflict was inevitable, and they therefore focused on mobilising the people for violence, and on developing some form of popular army or militia. They never got very far in this. For those who sincerely believed in the Chilean Road, either as a method on the way to conventional Soviet-style socialism, or as a means to a pluralistic and libertarian form of socialism, this was a mistaken approach. They needed to build a broad coalition for change in order to strengthen popular control over existing institutions, and make them function in new ways. In the military sphere instead of building an alternative armed force, what the left needed to do was strengthen the position of the constitu- tionalists and leftists within the armed forces while giving it a new constructive mission in society. The two visions within the left were always in competition and in many ways directly contradicted each other.

The contradiction was exacerbated by the way it was perceived outside the left. For many Chileans the 'traditional' framework of revolution was frightening. This fear of class violence was ably intensified by the right-wing media using propaganda designed in the United States, and which played on decades of negative reporting of the Soviet Union, Cuba and socialism in general. The fear was that at any moment the 'cloak' of democratic and pluralist socialism would be discarded for the 'reality' of a repressive authoritarian regime. Allende, it was feared, was a Chilean Kerensky. Because of this the left's language became increasingly important. So when the PS leadership declared in 1971 that 'Revolutionary violence is inevitable and legitimate [...] and is the only road that leads to the seizure of political and economic power' and that 'the PS considers the peaceful or legal forms of struggle limited instruments of a political process that leads us to the armed struggle' it struck icy fear into the hearts of many.[30] Gabriel Valdes, a leading Christian Democrat and Frei's former foreign minister, recalled the outgoing president Eduardo Frei telling Allende that he had become alienated from Chilean socialism since it was 'even more revolutionary and frenetic' than the communists, and that together they would end up 'exercising dictatorship'.[31] And he led the party that the Popular Unity needed to bring onside if they were to succeed. Within the left the apocalyptic language of the extremists may have been confined to a minority, but it was a vocal minority. Moreover, it was a minority that controlled much of the leadership of the main party of the UP government. While much of this violent language was for internal consumption, the effect on the UP's potential allies was understandable alarm. While they may not have feared Allende, they feared those who stood beside him. With both left and right aligned with regard to a traditional vision of revolution, this vision became the framework within which the Popular Unity government developed.

This issue was important because it formed the biggest barrier to cooperation with the PDC. While the Popular Unity programme was unique in its goals, the Christian Democrat programme had also promised many similar measures. It also envisioned the nationalisation of copper, the continuation of agrarian reform, and even mentioned the creation of 'Communitarian Socialism' with an enlarged state role in the economy. Meanwhile the Christian Democrats were torn. Much of the grassroots supported the Popular Unity process, while the leadership was consumed by arguments over the approach to take towards the government. Although Tomic and many others wanted to cooperate with the UP, Frei was still convinced that it was best that Allende's government fall as soon as possible. In the shadow of his public silence, and assisted by American dollars, the right wing of the PDC regrouped.[32] The left of the PDC, led by the party's candidate to the 1970 elections, Radimiro Tomic, Allende's old friend from the Senate, were convinced that Allende's proposed revolutionary path could not succeed without unity between left-wing Marxists and Christians. For both Tomic and Allende, Chile's problems could not be solved within capitalism.

Frei, Tomic and Allende knew that unless the UP could make some form of alliance with the PDC the Chilean political system would stall. In this system the president had broad powers but Congress could act as an effective block. There was no institution that could act as a referee if the two were at loggerheads, and therefore Allende knew that he had to nullify the threat of confrontation with Congress if his programme was to succeed. Chile was traditionally politically divided into 'three thirds'. This meant that no political force tended to absolutely dominate Congress, and required either a UP alliance with the PDC, or a plan which would enable the PDC to support those UP policies that were held broadly in common. Allende asked his personal advisers to come up with such a plan in mid October 1970. They presented it to him on the 25th of that month. The plan consisted of a referendum that would link the nationalisations of a list of large companies, and of copper and other natural resources, with the participation of workers in decision-making in housing and planning, and allow the president to dissolve parliament and call elections once during his term. The plan was intended to resolve the potential impasse between President and Congress, and it was hoped that by giving way on the ability to dissolve parliament, the idea would get broad support since there was great enthusiasm for the nationalisation of copper.[33]

Allende then took the two ideas to the Popular Unity leadership. Either an alliance needed to be made with the PDC while it was still led by its left wing, or the UP needed to try the referendum. The UP leadership rejected an alliance with the Christian Democrats because the PDC had been very hostile to the left during its mandate, and because of fears that it might be seen as a surrender to them. Furthermore, in the first weeks of the government it seemed the Christian Democrats might support the government without any formal alliance when the PDC voted to confirm Allende's victory, and then supported the nationalisation of copper. The referendum proposal also ran into stiff opposition with many worried that there was no way the

UP could get over 50 per cent in a referendum. By the third week of November the idea had been abandoned, although Allende tried to get versions of it approved several times in 1971 and early 1972. The failure to push through this proposal against the wishes of the UP leadership risked making the government hostage to the PDC. A few months later Allende asked the Christian Democrats to share the UP's 'historic responsibility', showing their 'accordance with the principle's and manifestos they offered the country so many times.'[34] Towards the end of 1971 Allende tried to consolidate an alliance with the PDC given the repeated rejection of a plebiscite by the UP leadership. He offered Tomic a ministerial role, but Tomic rejected it feeling that he and the left wing of his party had been hung out to dry by the UP leadership. Soon afterwards Tomic lost control of the PDC, no doubt aided by the funds the CIA was disbursing to Frei and his supporters.[35]

Despite this, one of the UP's most important victories was achieved with unanimous support in Congress, showing how far Allende and the left had managed to make their proposals a centrepiece of popular common sense. Demand for nationalisation had become so widespread that the bill passed unanimously. Over 30 years after it was first proposed, Allende's dream had been realised. The decree nationalising the copper industry was signed on 22 November 1970. It was in effect, the foundation of modern Chile, and perhaps the Popular Unity's most lasting legacy, since copper has been the largest contributor to state coffers ever since.

Allende called the day the decree came into effect, 11 July 1971, 'the day of national dignity' and said that it marked the moment that Chile started out on its road to its second, definitive independence. Allende always had an eye for historical symbolism, and he spoke his words in the city of Rancagua, the site of a famous 1814 battle in Chile's wars of Independence, and a few miles from the famous El Teniente copper mine. In his speech Allende explained to the people the problems that the nationalisation process had encountered and would yet have to confront thanks to the foreign copper companies. These copper companies had begun a race to get as much copper ore out before the nationalisation took place. They stopped investing in machinery and left rubble in the mines. Furthermore, the US mining experts who had managed much of the industry began to leave Chile, leaving unqualified Chileans to deal with the mess.[36] Two teams of mining specialists from France and the Soviet Union confirmed that the mines were in a sorry state, and that it would take heavy investment just to get them up and running at capacity.

Another key point in the UP programme was the completion of the land reform begun in the 1960s. While the nationalisation of copper would allow the government to plan future economic growth based on the production of copper and other minerals. The agrarian reform would enable small and medium scale farmers, alongside state-run and collective farms, to produce enough food for domestic needs and for export. Together they would create an internal market for Chilean industry. The nationalisation of copper would be combined with the creation of an international copper organisation aimed at regulating prices to the advantage of copper producers. Copper, the wage of Chile, together with Chile's other minerals, would fund the vast transformation of society that Allende and the Popular Unity planned.

The economic aspects of the programme were highly optimistic, and made several assumptions that underestimated the potential effect of political events.[37] It was assumed that nationalisation and a progressive wage policy would soon create bulging state coffers and an enlarged internal market. However, the nationalised mines needed massive investment. Wage increases allowed people to spend on food, but agricultural production was disrupted by the agrarian reform and the combination created shortages and inflation. It was also assumed that the Chilean elite would take advantage of an enlarged market to invest in business, but instead many began moving money abroad, fearing further nationalisations. In combination with the problems created in the economy, the imposition of price controls also helped enlarge the black market. The government could have dealt with these problems, but in combination with growing political polarisation, foreign interference and an economic blockade the situation began to spin out of control.

Despite this, with the opposition in disarray, during its first year Allende's government made many advances in its legislative programme, and its economic strategy showed promising signs of success. Inflation was brought under control, from over 30 per cent to under 15 per cent, and GDP grew by nearly 8 per cent (in comparison to less than 3 per cent under the previous government). Industrial production, mining and agriculture all showed increases. Some problems were beginning to show, such as the increasing shortages of food products thanks to increased consumption, but the government was still optimistic. Chile was living an unprecedented boom with masses of people having access to more and better food and consumer goods.

This optimism was bolstered by the results of the April 1971 municipal elections when the UP increased its support to over 50 per cent, it was an unprecedented success achieved despite American financial support for opposition media and candidates. An improvement in the share of the vote was unheard of in Chilean politics and it moved Allende to push the UP to call a plebiscite on designing a new constitution for Chile. However, most within both the Socialist and Communist party leaderships opposed it, fearing that despite the municipal results, the UP would lose a plebiscite that went beyond economic measures and proposed a massive restructuring of the political system.[38] The idea was shelved. This period was the zenith of the Popular Unity government. It appeared to be in control. It was also the highpoint of Allende's life, the culmination of his life's work. The economy was booming, society was enjoying a revolutionary 'fiesta' of participation and a cultural carnival. It was not to last long. The UP still had no majority in Congress and this gave the PDC the key to the situation.

For much of 1971 the Christian Democrats wavered on the position they ought to take with regard to the UP. For some, the PDC had to judge each piece of legislation independently. Others wanted to bring the PDC into a total opposition, allying it with the right. In December 1970 the former position won out temporarily, and therefore until mid way through 1971 the PDC de-facto cooperated with the UP in Congress. This position was even made official in a PDC national congress in May 1971. Allende knew that the UP needed to build on this and proposed that the UP not present a candidate for the July 1971 Valparaiso senate by-election.[39] If the UP promised to vote for a PDC candidate it would provide tangible proof to Christian Democrat waverers that allying with the government could bring them benefits, helping to prevent them from being led into the arms of the right by Frei's supporters within the party. Instead the Socialist Party leadership insisted on putting forward a Socialist candidate. The opportunity and the election were lost. The PDC candidate won, supported by the right.

The Christian Democrats' rightward turn had already begun. On 8 June Frei's friend and former Interior Minister Edmundo Perez Zujovic was gunned down by members of an obscure extremist group called the VOP (Popular Organised Vanguard). It claimed to have killed Zujovic in revenge for a 1969 massacre of unarmed shanty town dwellers in Puerto Montt, but Zujovic had also been a leading proponent of a PDC alliance with the UP. The killing had a massive effect on the PDC. Rushing to express his solidarity, Allende called it a 'crime against Chile', declaring three days of national mourning. He said that the killing had been intended to 'create a climate of confusion, of mistrust and of political vengeance against the Popular Government', but Frei accused the Popular Unity and Allende of 'bringing violence to Chile', and the opposition media took advantage of the murder to excoriate the left in general, blaming Allende for his amnesty of political prisoners, including some members of the VOP earlier in the year.[40] Despite this, several leading Christian Democrats believed the killing to have been motivated from abroad given its suspicious timing just after the PDC had agreed to cooperate with the UP and just before the by-election.[41] The assassination also came at a time when the CIA was spending large amounts of money on the Freista sectors of the PDC, in an effort to turn it into an outright opposition party.[42] Whatever the truth, the killing of Zujovic, and failure to support the PDC in Valparaiso were major factors in turning the Christian Democrats against the government. The right of the Party was also helped when a group of left-wing PDC congressmen, against Allende's advice, split from the PDC creating a new party called the Left Christians (IC). They were accepted into the UP, where they soon took up radical positions. This wing of the UP together with the MIR, were active opponents of reaching agreement with the PDC, and they repeatedly blocked Allende's efforts. In July 1971 the PDC voted to replace the UP President of Congress with one of their own. The phase of cooperation was over.

The failing relationship with the PDC was not completely the fault of the extreme leftists within the UP, but they undoubtedly hampered Allende's ability to lead the process forward and contributed to the deteriorating situation by attacking the government strategy from the left, while it was increasingly under siege from abroad and from the right. Already by the end of 1971 these attacks were beginning to spin the Popular Unity process out of control. Thus, although Allende thought the balance of the first year of his government was positive, his anniversary speech noted some major issues, several of which had to do with the effect that the extreme left was having on the process. 'We need public order [in order] to change the structures [...] we are against the indiscriminate seizures of farms that create anarchy in production and end up pitching peasant against peasant.' Knowing the respect that many in the extreme left had for the revolutionary classics, a leaning that Allende himself did not share ('We set a lot more store by actions than by words here' he said to Debray), Allende quoted Lenin to the 'minority groups' who pushed for ever more radical action. 'By revolutionary phrase-making we mean the repetition of revolutionary slogans irrespective of objective circumstances at a given turn invents. The slogans are superb, alluring, intoxicating, but there are no grounds for them.'[43]

The problem was that similar views to those of the 'minority groups' that Allende mentioned were present within Allende's own Socialist Party, and within some of the smaller parties of the Popular Unity coalition. In early 1971 the Socialist Party had elected a leadership that was committed to making real the resolutions of the 1967 Congress, electing Carlos Altamirano – a tall, bespectacled firebrand – to put them into effect. That

Congress had passed resolutions that directly contradicted Allende's Chilean Road to Socialism, stating for example that 'Revolutionary violence is inevitable and legitimate', that 'we consider the national bourgeoisie is an ally of imperialism and is in fact its tool' and that the 'so-called left wing of the PDC is serving as a screen for the right'. This leadership clearly had little faith in the Chilean Road to Socialism. It did not want an alliance with the Christian Democrats and instead leaned towards the like-minded revolutionaries outside the UP coalition, pushing for confrontation. These positions were so influential within the PS at the time that even within Allende's family there was much sympathy for them. Beatriz, Allende's daughter, had been trained in Cuba and had a close relationship with the MIR leadership. Although Beatriz remained in the PS she shared the MIR's apocalyptic vision of the future, and like many of her generation she was highly critical of her father's 'reformist' politics.

Despite their political differences and the difference in age, Allende had developed a close friendship with Altamirano. Allende liked debate, and Altamirano provided it, and they also shared a similar social background. The two men were both former athletes and it is likely that Allende saw something of his own impatient youth in Altamirano.[44] Allende probably thought experience might mellow Altamirano, and that he would be able to control him if not.[45] In the La Serena Congress Allende threw his weight behind preventing Altamirano's rival, Aniceto Rodríguez, from retaining his position as General Secretary. Although they shared a faith in the potential of the electoral road, Allende probably suspected Rodríguez's political judgement, since he had supported Ibañez's second government. In 1970 Rodríguez had exacerbated these concerns by heavily pressuring Allende to give him the Ministry of Interior. Allende refused fearing it would concentrate too much power in his hands.[46] Allende feared that supporting Rodríguez would strengthen the right wing of the Socialist Party. Since the Popular Front had been brought down by a rightward shift in the leadership of the Socialist Party, Allende probably sought to avoid a similar mistake. Yet Allende's decision to block Rodríguez opened the road for Altamirano, who later seriously damaged possibilities of an alliance with the PDC when, throughout 1972 and 1973, he pushed for the creation of alternative mechanisms of power, striving to push the Chilean road to socialism into the channel of a 'traditional' revolution.

In this, Altamirano and the people he represented in the PS were following a similar path to that offered by the MIR outside the Popular Unity. Here, too, the MIR was arguing for the radicalisation of the process, carrying out the seizure of small farms and small businesses by landless labourers and workers and trying to develop a military force and mobilising the people around confrontation. For the Communists the frustration with this position was intense. One Communist trade unionist expressed it succinctly: 'The youngsters of the MIR want confrontation now. I can't accept that they attack us communists as bourgeois and unrevolutionary. We have fought for years. We have suffered repression. The working class has been dying for a hundred years to reach a situation like this and the MIR wants to throw it all out of the window in three days of fighting.'[47] But the idea that 'the revolution' could be made quickly was attractive to many, especially the young. Ironically, after Allende's election the MIR had begun to abandon its original political-military structures and started working more like a political party, organising in shantytowns and some rural areas. However this mobilisation took place outside the state, and often in opposition to it, seeing Allende and the Popular Unity as 'reformist'.

At the end of 1972, Fidel Castro, one of the icons of the extreme left in Chile, arrived for a visit scheduled to last ten days, but which extended to over three weeks. It was Castro's first visit to mainland Latin America since the revolution and he revelled in the chance to get to know Chile. Castro's visit provoked an outraged response from the Chilean right, for whom he was a terrifying figure. 'Never has a more open and barefaced intervention in the internal affairs of a country been seen as in Chile by that "Caribbean adventurer"', said one military officer later linked to the coup.[48] The close relations between Allende and Castro seemed to them to confirm that no matter what Allende said, his goal was to turn Chile into another Cuba. Castro tried to support Allende and the 'Chilean Road'. In public he exhorted the masses to unite behind Allende's government, and in private meetings with the MIR leadership Castro also warned them that in Chile the revolution would be 'made by Allende, or by no-one.' But Castro's very presence increased the polarisation, and he was able to see with his own eyes how it developed, and it worried him. Two days before he left the opposition organised a 'March of the Empty Pots', where women from the wealthy neighbourhoods, accompanied by their maids, marched, led and flanked by detachments of baton- and chain-wielding young men from the fascist paramilitary group 'Fatherland and Liberty'. The march ended in violence as demonstrators attacked offices belonging to the Radical Party and the Communist Youth. 'Fascism is trying to advance and win ground among the middle classes and seize the streets', Castro warned.[49]

Earlier in the year, in March 1972, documents were released showing US transnational ITT's efforts to undermine the government, highlighting links between the CIA, US business and anti-UP groups in Chile. Allende failed to crack down on them. During the same year the right-wing media, now largely funded from abroad, openly called for a coup in violation of Chilean law, and yet again Allende did not act against them. As President, Allende prioritised the toleration of dissent over the need to crack down. In fact it was difficult for Allende to repress seditious activity without undermining his government's democratic credentials, which were vital if he hoped to create an alliance with the PDC. As the experience with the judiciary showed, Allende could not rely on it to appropriately punish those who were brought before the law. Nor could he promote the organisation of a popular response to right-wing violence without destroying the already difficult path being followed by the 'Chilean road'. Allende had to rely, therefore, on the institutions of the state, and he did institute a state of emergency in Santiago after the March of the Empty Pots. In his farewell speech Castro noted that revolutions needed 'audacity, audacity and audacity' in order to succeed. For him, the Popular Unity's (and Allende's) commitment to pluralism and free speech were translating into giving the opposition a free hand to do what it liked – Allende needed to be more decisive in dealing with his opponents and for this reason Castro privately encouraged the Popular Unity to take steps to prepare for the violence that the reactionary elite and its allies in the United States were clearly preparing.[50]

The right was definitely on the move. Two days after the March of the Empty Pots, the Christian Democrats in Congress voted to impeach Allende's Minister of Interior, José Tohá on the false grounds that he was supporting paramilitary groups. In January 1972 the right-wing National Party (PN) called for a united front of all non-Marxist parties. In February 1972 the National Party and the PDC allied during by-elections in two provinces, forming the basis of a political alliance that would last until the coup. In March leading figures from across the opposition – the PDC, the PN, church leaders, business leaders and members of the judiciary met to plan coordinated actions for the future. In April a 'March for Democracy' united the PDC, the National Party and other opposition forces to protest what Patricio Aylwin, the PDC President of the Senate, called 'the threats and violations that [our] democratic rights are being subjected to increasingly and more openly every day.' In answer to Allende's calls for moderation he warned, 'we will be inflexible in exercising our rights.' The Popular Unity responded with an even larger mobilisation where Allende underlined that those gathered had come to defend 'authentic democracy and authentic liberty.' Yet the possibility of a political agreement still existed. In August the government was a hair's breadth from signing an agreement with the PDC over a reform to property law that would stabilise the chaos around the three areas of property (state, mixed and private). On the day the agreement was to be signed, Eduardo Frei rang from Europe, where he was meeting the leaders of the Christian Democrat international, and ordered two PDC senators not to attend the signing, meaning that the Senate did not reach quorum and the agreement sank.[51]

At the same time university campuses and the streets bore witness to growing violence between youths affiliated to political groups. Sometimes the fighting was between left and right, at other times even between leftist groups. Behind the façade of violence and political obstructionism in Congress the right made more use of its wealth and its extensive social networks to develop plans to overthrow Allende. At the same time the CIA, US transnationals and even European money contributed to the opposition's development. In August 1972 the parliamentary opposition united in a 'Democratic Confederation', but just as important were the secret meetings and dinners. The opposition was becoming more united and more than willing to use violence.

In October 1972 the National Confederation of Transport began the national strike that they had begun planning in March, using the pretext of opposition to the government's proposal to create a state-owned transport company for the far south. The strike was organised and supported by business leaders, the National Party and the Christian Democrats, and largely funded by CIA monies.[52] Hundreds of lorries were stopped and disabled in strategic locations, blocking transport hubs and causing shortages and chaos. The truck owners attacked strike-breakers and 'Fatherland and Liberty' carried out other violent attacks. Allende's response was to declare a state of emergency in several provinces, and to rally popular support. Hundreds of thousands of people mobilised voluntarily in supply depots and at railway stations to allow the flow of food and other products to continue. The government also made use of a network of computers akin to an early internet that had been installed by British scientist Stafford Beer. The system provided a rudimentary method of linking together factories and ministries in order to provide an accurate picture of the state of the economy. Cybersyn, as the system was known, helped the government to allocate resources effectively in the face of the blockade.[53] The government tried to negotiate with the strikers, but the problem was that the strikers' demands were largely political. Allende persisted. On 1 November the government brought the top ranks of the armed forces in to manage the Ministry of Interior, the Ministry of Public Works and the Ministry of Mining. The negotiations continued, and after an agreement not to prosecute those involved, the strikers brought their actions to an end. Enormous damage had been done to the economy.

Furthermore, the inclusion of the military in government was highly controversial, and for some it marked the end of the socialist stage of Allende's government. It did nothing to resolve the debate over whether to supersede the institutions of the state, or rely on them. New organisations of the working class had been key in overcoming the challenge of the 'bosses' strike', but they also threatened to further divide the forces supporting the government. These organisations became known as 'industrial belts' and were a form of popular participation and organisation that developed spontaneously and outside the traditional trade union and party structures. Their autonomy threatened the grand strategy being followed by Allende and yet were also a potential source of non-party popular support for the process. It opened the question of whether to rely on the institutions of the state or supersede them, a question that became increasingly divisive. Initially Allende and the Communists opposed them for threatening to create a parallel trade union movement. Then they switched to trying to subordinate them to the CUT, and to the government programme.[54] From this point on the MIR began to increase its activity in promoting 'popular power' and land seizures, and the UP was paralysed by the debate over strategy.

Allende took advantage of the lull that followed the truck owners' strike to head on a short tour of Latin America, also visiting the Soviet Union before returning via New York where he addressed the General Assembly of the UN. Abroad he found respite from the relentless pressure at home, and was able to work at improving Chile's international situation. In the Soviet Union Allende was looking for ways of shoring up Chile's economy which was being put to the sword by a combination of elite intransigence and US government and private sector efforts to 'make it scream'. A drop in copper prices and the natural dislocation caused by the UP's structural reforms also took their toll. Allende was to be disappointed. The Soviets and various East European countries had already provided credits and assistance, but some had been left unused. Furthermore, for the Soviet leadership détente with the United States was a priority, and they had little confidence in the Chilean road to socialism given the divisions within the Chilean left. Brezhnev and others were also sceptical of the UP government's apparent confidence in the armed forces. Furthermore, Allende was asking for the Soviet Union to grant aid on conditions it had not given any other developing country.[55] Unsurprisingly, Allende failed to receive the economic support he had been seeking. In Latin America his reception was better, but the economic possibilities were virtually nil. The region's economies were not integrated, with the vast majority of their trade aimed northwards. This left him denouncing the intervention against his country in the UN, 'we find ourselves facing forces that operate in the shadows, without a flag, with powerful weapons and posted in the most varied places of influence', 'we are victims of almost imperceptible actions, generally disguised with phrases and declarations that express respect for the sovereignty and dignity of our country.' Unfortunately for Allende, the international community that gave his speech a standing ovation was not in a position to help. The Chilean popular movement with Allende at its head had to face its enemies alone.

Figure 6.3   Salvador Allende with Fidel Castro during his visit to Cuba, December 1972.

The only hope for success lay in reaching an understanding with the Christian Democrats and Allende fought tooth and nail to achieve it. Right until the end Allende was confident that he would be able to find a way out by doing so.[56] In March 1972 Allende asked his Justice Minister to open channels with the PDC, but the talks foundered. From mid 1972 onwards his government was increasingly on the defensive. The possibility of an agreement with the PDC remained, but like a will-o'-the-wisp, every time it seemed on the verge of being signed, it receded into the distance. The games continued when Patricio Aylwin became president of the PDC in May 1973, although Aylwin was a hard-line opponent of the UP, and he gradually sidelined the left-wing majority within the PDC. Allende refused to let the right wing of the PDC win. An agreement with Aylwin could bring the entire PDC on board. Allende went over Aylwin's head and convinced Cardinal Raul Silva Henriquez to talk to Aylwin. The Cardinal pushed hard for Aylwin to come to an agreement with Allende. In July and August 1973 talks between the two took place, at the same time as the PDC continued to block the government in Congress and a sector of the PS rejected any retreat on the government's programme. Allende knew it was time for desperate measures. 'I am in your hands' he told Gabriel Valdes, in words he could easily have addressed to Carlos Altamirano. 'One hundred years of workers' struggle and social progress depend on you.' On 10 September, the day before the coup Allende received a final 'no' from the PDC, forcing him to play his last remaining card – that of a plebiscite on the constitutional reforms proposed by the UP, and in effect a plebiscite on his government.

7

The Coup

The inability to resolve the crisis in the political arena made the position of the military increasingly important. The Chilean armed forces were proud of their professionalism and their subordination to constitutional power, but in reality throughout their history they had played an important role in shaping the Chilean state and on occasion, in defining political outcomes – as in the 1920s and 1930s – but had then acquiesced to a much-reduced role.[1] In the 1960s the military command underwent a generational change in which the influence of General Ibañez faded, replaced by US training programmes that introduced a concept of national security which identified communism as a key threat. In an environment of cuts and low social esteem the national security role provided an attractive raison d'etre for some within the armed forces.[2] On the other hand, Chile's chronic socio-economic underdevelopment and the nation's subsequent military weakness influenced a strong 'developmentalist' strain of thought, too. The top brass were also affected by military involvement in politics elsewhere, from Nasser's Egypt to the Latin American coups. Such examples contrasted with the neglect that the Chilean military were subjected to by the political elite, leading to increasing resentment.[3] Therefore by the time Allende came to power competing ideas regarding the legitimacy of military intervention, and the solutions to national problems, existed within the armed forces.

A 1969 'Synthesis of the National Situation' written by the General Staff noted that 80 per cent of armed forces' personnel were of 'non-Marxist centre-left political tendencies' while the remaining 20 per cent were a 'small sector of the top and high ranking officer corps of rightist inclinations, and another, also small sector within the medium and lower ranks of the officer corps that is infiltrated by Marxist propaganda.' While the numbers seemed stacked in favour of the left, in reality the concentration of right-wingers at the top of the hierarchy made all the difference. A constitutionalist officer, Colonel Pickering, recalled officer reactions to Allende's election as 'indifference among a few; surprise, disappointment, irritation – and even fear among the rest.'[4]

Right from the beginning seditious groups and the CIA began making contact with the military to provoke them into action against the Popular Unity. One opposition group linked to the navy formed a sailing club, where retired and off duty officers could innocently mix with the civilian groups plotting against the Popular Unity. Others shared friendships and family connections. These spaces provided the arena for the discussions of what needed to be done to help unseat Allende's government. Initial contacts showed that naval officers in Valparaiso were motivated for a coup, but the reverse was true of the army. Even Pinochet, who later led the coup, was not involved in the plotting at this stage. In these early days the anti-Allende forces in the military were on the back foot. Some were fearful of civil war – one high ranking naval officer recalled a secret intelligence report that said that the 1970 election results had provoked shouts of 'Viva Comrade Allende!' in the majority of the barracks in the country.[5] Others were forced to wait for a better opportunity after the assassination of General Rene Schneider on 22 October. In the investigation that followed it was clear that several senior officers were involved in the plot, among them two generals and a former commander of the navy, all with links to the civilian elite and to the CIA. Schneider's killing and its fallout prevented any further action by the military opposition for a while.

In their 1969 Synthesis the General Staff had noted that whatever government took over in 1970, it had to ensure new political, economic and social transformations but 'without allowing the penetration of Marxism to the sources of power.' Yet this was exactly what the Popular Unity aimed at doing. In 1970 the Operations and Intelligence Secretariat of the Army produced a report on the upcoming elections. In this report the military predicted the political tensions that would be produced, each outcome would result in military intervention. If the right won the left would turn to subversion and to contain it the armed forces would be used. Meanwhile, if Allende won the report predicted an initial period of calm, since 'the public forces antagonistic to him [Allende] have not yet showed any pronounced tendency to provoke public disorder.' However, this period would not last long and would depend on the government's capacity to control 'extremist elements' outside and inside the government. If these extremists began to act, then the government would have two options – to seek an alliance with other political forces and use repression; or it would react 'timidly without trying to control popular excesses.' In either case, the armed forces would need to prepare 'a long and costly deployment' to enforce internal order.[6]

The army report was right. With the constellation of forces conspiring to destabilise the new government it would not be long before social unrest became a regular occurrence. As politics became stalemated in Congress, it spilled out onto the streets and the countryside. It seeped into the lives of every Chilean in the queues for food, in disturbances at university, in people's voluntary labour, in the fields and in the factories. It was scrawled on the walls of the cities, and on the rocks of Chile's mountain roads. Politics was optimistically and colourfully painted on the river embankments, and city walls, and angrily blaring from the television and the radio with the opposition calling for Chileans to 'gather their rage'. As Allende said: 'every day, in every minute two worlds are in confrontation, two concepts of social order and human coexistence.' One was the world that 'has existed.' The other world was the new revolutionary process that Chileans had to build together in the face of the desperate resistance of the 'structures, institutions, classes and men that have the continuity of their privileges threatened.'[7] In these circumstances it was inevitable that the armed forces became a political factor.

The problem for Allende was that his programme of transformations had no active policy for how to accommodate a military politicisation. The assumption was that if the Popular Unity provided economic growth and social development this would translate into greater national 'power' and therefore please the military. As he expressed to the High Command in 1972, 'there are no powerful armed forces if there are peoples decimated by illness or punished by ignorance. There are no powerful armed forces in countries that are economically, culturally and sometimes, all too often, politically dependent.'[8] Greater control over the nation's resources would allow the government to improve pay and conditions, modernise military infrastructure, and provide more modern equipment. Its incorporation into the process of development would also resolve the military's political frustrations and gradually make it identify with the problems of the people. Allende's project envisioned a medium to long-term transformation of the armed forces alongside the transformation of society and the state.

For this strategy to succeed the government needed to emphasise the positive traditions of the armed forces, the government's historical continuity with the fight for independence, and crucially prevent the development of an alternative military force by the left. The military's tradition of constitutionalism thus became a keystone of the process, which Allende tried to encourage by not interfering in military appointments or promotions. Unfortunately these efforts were undermined by a section of his own party which was bent on creating its 'own military force', and the MIR also claimed the right to build a 'popular army'. Whilst in reality these efforts were miniscule and largely symbolic, they were magnified out of all proportion by the opposition-controlled and CIA funded media, and by the militants themselves.[9] Many officers believed the hype, fearing the development of 'popular militias' and a potential civil war. But this was not the only problem. For any military the question of 'order' is crucial. For many officers, as the 1970 intelligence report predicted, the government was being lenient on 'extremist elements', and was in their view promoting social unrest, which in turn weakened the nation in the face of potential threats from abroad. Furthermore, the government's foreign policy, in particular its relations with socialist countries, further increased the potential threat to the country from its neighbours and the United States.[10] To make things worse the increasing economic disorder was also weakening the country's ability to go to war.

For practical and ideological reasons the military opposition could justify its position. The overthrow of Allende was a matter of national salvation, for the survival of the '*patria*'.

However, the military opposition was not able to act while the army high command remained loyal to the constitution. The position of the army was crucial to the success of any coup, and within the army the attitude of the Commander in Chief, the commander of the Santiago garrison and the commander of the military schools were critical. The coup plotters controlled none of these posts until days before the coup. For two years the coup plotters had been unable to gain a strong foothold within the army, but from early 1973 onwards their position grew in strength in parallel with the growth of the rest of the opposition. In October 1972 the armed forces helped the government weather the transport owners' strike, and the following month Allende incorporated the top brass into his government, giving General Carlos Prats, Commander of the Army, the Ministry of Interior. While this temporarily quieted the opposition, it also overtly politicised the military. Then on 29 July 1973 the army's 2nd Armoured Regiment staged an abortive coup attempt. After some fighting the rebellious troops were brought under control by loyal forces. Carlos Prats and other constitutional officers played a notable role and were lauded by Allende. However, the 'Tanquetazo' showed that the opposition within the armed forces had re-emerged from the shadows. Days later, on 9 August, the top brass were reluctantly brought into the government again.

The pressures on the military were immense and they gradually bore fruit. General Sepulveda later recalled that 'for weeks, every day, the men received this pressure [from the opposition], through their wife, their children, their relatives and friends, with regard to the situation they were living and how long were we going to tolerate it.'[11] Those in important commands were particularly targeted. The constitutionalist officers were forced out of their positions at the top of the hierarchy by a virtual rebellion of lower ranking officers committed to the coup. On 17 August General Ruiz, Commander of the Air Force and Minister of Transport, resigned his ministerial post. At a dinner that night Allende desperately tried to convince him to stay, but Ruiz was adamant. 'You are no longer a friend and have lost my trust', Allende told him, rising from the table.[12] He replaced Ruiz with his second-in-command, General Leigh. Ruiz was not the only one considering resignation. Carlos Prats was also torn. If he resigned then he 'had the contemptuous role of rats when they flee a sinking ship', but if he remained the attacks against him would increase.[13]

The situation required decisive action to be taken against the coup plotters within and outside the armed forces, but this was not forthcoming because it was feared that it would provoke a coup. Prats told Allende that he would need to fire '12–15 Generals and this would provoke civil war.'[14] Allende's hopes hinged on a deal with the Christian Democrats, since if this could be achieved it would pull the rug from under the military plotters. He was not prepared to consider illegal action. 'We cannot break legality because we are the government. We have always fought for the law to be respected because in a democratic state it prevents despotism and arbitrariness, avoiding Chileans killing each other, and guaranteeing the conquests made by the workers', he said.[15] Unfortunately, the opposition preferred breaking the system to preserve their power, and they did not mind killing Chileans to do it.

On 26 July 1973, after returning home from a reception at the Cuban embassy, Allende's naval aide, Commander Arturo Araya, was shot and killed. Allende was distraught. Over the past two years they had developed a close friendship. Allende rushed to the hospital, donned a white surgeon's overall and desperately massaged Araya's heart. When Araya failed to revive, Allende looked up, and with tears in his eyes said, 'Gentlemen, Commander Araya has died. This is fascism!'[16] Allende appointed a team of investigators from each branch of the armed forces and the police to find the perpetrators and the next day the Carabineros reported having arrested a member of the Socialist Party who confessed that he had been involved. The suspect alleged a group of Cubans and the leader of Allende's GAP security team had been involved. The media created a scandal by picking up the accusation. The Carabineros then denied an arrest had been made. Then the investigations police

interviewed the witness and found that he had been severely
tortured into giving a false confession. The investigation showed
the involvement of 'Fatherland and Liberty', although the
murderers have never been found.[17] Then in August 1973 sailors
from Valparaiso requested a secret meeting with Altamirano and
Oscar Garreton, the leader of the MAPU, where they denounced
coup preparations in the navy. The sailors involved were then
arrested by their superiors and brutally tortured for alleged links
to 'extremist organisations'. Reports of their treatment reached
the government, but sticking to the law, Allende called for an
official investigation without acting to punish the coup plotters
saying to Carlos Altamirano, 'we can't base an accusation
against the high command on the testimony of some sailors.'[18]
The pressures on the government grew by the day, and in mid
August Allende began to keep a small bottle of Valium by his
bed.[19] In a July speech to the workers of the CUT he admitted
that often 'doubt and bitterness tighten my throat', but he steeled
himself by remembering 'the ordinary woman who believed in
me', and 'the children of my country', no doubt recalling the
injustice, poverty and desperation he had witnessed so often
during his life.[20]

Meanwhile the pressure and the media attacks on the constitutionalist officers continued. Prats was a particular target of
these. On 20 August military wives demonstrated outside the
Ministry of Defence, on 21 August they did so outside his house
where he was ill with flu. Over 1,000 irate women screamed
abuse, hurling stones at his home. Prats ordered the police not
to clear the road, fearing that they might injure some of the
demonstrators. The following day Prats asked his fellow officers
to express their solidarity with him, but Pinochet returned with
the news that many of his comrades had refused to do so.[21]
On 24 August the isolated Prats resigned from the army – it
was not, after all, 'his revolution.'[22] He hoped this would give
Allende time to reach an agreement with the PDC, and at the
same time avoid staining his hands with blood. Unfortunately,
Prats' resignation removed 'the main factor mitigating against
a coup.'[23] It was now a matter of time.

Prats was replaced by his trusted second-in-command, Augusto Pinochet. Even on 9 September his position remained unclear to the other plotters. Without his inclusion the likelihood of a civil war increased since it might split the army. Yet on 10 September Pinochet officially joined the coup and took it over. Pinochet first appeared on the CIA radar in August 1971, when a report stated that both his wife and son were 'turning against the Allende government' and hoped to influence Pinochet. In March 1972 another CIA source stated that Pinochet was involved with coup plotters linked to General Canales, and in September 1972 Pinochet was reported to be 'harbouring second thoughts' about Allende, but there is no evidence of his coordinating with other officers.[24] We may never know if Pinochet was merely playing it safe, giving the appearance of loyalty to both sides before making a final decision. He may have seen the government in disarray over how to confront a coup, its inability to agree on a plebiscite and calculated that it could never win a confrontation.[25] He had no reason to stay loyal to Allende for, as he said to Arellano on 8 September, 'I'm no Marxist, dammit!' However, once Pinochet came down on the side of the coup, victory was almost assured.

Admiral Montero, the head of the navy, remained, but he was isolated and due to be replaced on 12 September by Admiral Merino, a committed coup plotter. On the night before the coup a team of sailors cut Montero's phone lines and disabled his car. By one means or another in early September the top constitutionalists in the army had been isolated or removed.

The coup plotters had set a date, 11 September 1973. Starting at 6 a.m. naval forces would take the city of Valparaiso and cut communications there and in Santiago. At 8 a.m. the army would move in Santiago. An inner circle of troops from the Santiago garrison would overthrow the government, and take over energy, water and telecommunications installations to prevent workers from disabling them. Columns from outside the city would then eliminate any resistance in the outskirts. The air force was on hand to destroy government radio stations, and if necessary the Moneda palace and any points of resistance. Pinochet based himself in the army communications centre in the foothills of the Andes on the outskirts of the city. Others took up position just opposite the Moneda palace in the Ministry of Defence – three floors of which were dominated by the US Military Advisory Group. Reports of strange troop movements in Valparaiso and towns near Santiago began coming in to the UP party leaderships and to the government. The Defence Minister, Orlando Letelier, later killed in Washington by Pinochet's secret service, was the first government figure detained when he arrived to clarify the situation in his Ministry.

Reports of suspicious troops movements began to arrive at midnight. Allende was woken at about 4 a.m. He began trying to find out what was happening. Eventually he decided to go to the Moneda, where he arrived at about 7.20 a.m., wearing charcoal grey trousers, and a turtleneck jumper covered by a tweed jacket, accompanied by a group of his bodyguards and some Carabineros. He carried an AKM rifle given to him by Fidel Castro during his 1971 visit, and headed straight for his office, relieved that the long wait was over. He called Tencha, his wife of 34 years: 'Tencha, the navy has rebelled... I don't know if we'll be able to withstand it.' They bid each other farewell, not knowing it would be for the last time. At 7.55 a.m. Allende addressed a nation uncertain of what was happening. Many felt relief that the army had acted at last. Many more felt dread and trepidation. In a calm voice Allende informed the people that part of the navy had mutinied, and that the city of Valparaiso had been taken, but he expressed his hope, his certainty that the 'soldiers of the fatherland' would know their duty. 'I am here, and I will stay here defending the government I represent by the will of the people.' In the meantime, the people, the workers had to mobilise themselves to their workplaces in order to defend their government. Beatriz, his daughter, arrived – six months pregnant and insisting on helping to defend the Moneda. She had military training after all. She called Miguel Enriquez, the leader of the MIR, to whom Allende sent a message – 'Miguel, it's your turn now.' Throughout the early morning friends, comrades and colleagues arrived to the Moneda.

Allende called the various branches of the armed forces, and at 8.15 a.m. he again addressed the nation. He confirmed the rebellion in Valparaiso, but said that he had ordered loyal troops

to the city and he expected that 'The loyal forces [...] alongside
the organised workers will crush the fascist coup threatening the
fatherland.' But as the military edicts began to come over the air,
he and his followers in the Moneda soon realised that not a single
unit was staying loyal. He again addressed the country. 'In this
edict they demand the President resign. I will not do it. I notify
the country of the incredible attitude of soldiers that are breaking
their word and their commitments.' He reminded the country
that General José Maria Sepulveda, the official commander of
the Carabineros, was by his side. A jet passed overhead. Allende
continued, 'In this instant planes are passing over the Moneda.
They will probably machine gun it. We are serene and calm.
Our holocaust will mark the infamy of those who betray the
fatherland and the people.'

At 8.30 a.m. the first military pronouncement made clear that
Pinochet was part of the sedition. At 8.45 a.m. Allende picked
up the phone and made another address to the nation. 'The
situation is critical', he said:

> We are facing a coup in which the majority of the armed forces are
> participating. In this dark hour I want to remind you of the words I said in
> 1971, I say them calmly, with total tranquillity – I do not have the makings
> of an apostle or a messiah. I don't have the makings of a martyr; I am
> a social fighter fulfilling a task given to me by the people. But let those
> who want to rewind history and ignore the will of the majority of Chile
> know, without being a martyr, I will not take a single step backwards.
> Let them know it, let them hear it, let it be deeply engraved in them – I
> will leave the Moneda when I have fulfilled the mandate that the Chilean
> people gave me.

He continued,

> I will defend this government and I will defend this revolution because it
> is the mandate given to me by the people. I have no alternative. Only by
> riddling me with bullets will they be able to impede the will to complete
> the programme of the people. If they kill me, the people will continue
> its route, it will follow its road with the difference maybe that things will
> be much, much harder, much more violent, because it will be a clear,

objective lesson to the masses that these people stop at nothing. I had that possibility accounted for. I do not offer it or facilitate it. The social process will not disappear because a leader disappears. It may be delayed, it may be prolonged, but at the end it cannot be halted.

Allende finished and drummed his fingers on his desk muttering 'three traitors, three traitors...'.[26]

One of Allende's comrades asked if they should try to contact Prats. Allende made a disappointed gesture and said, 'Let's not talk about him.' In any case Prats preferred to lie low rather than risk a civil war. At the end of 1972 he had told a meeting of generals that a civil war would mean at least 100,000 and possibly up to 1 million dead. On 7 July Allende had invited Prats for dinner, where he asked him whether he thought part of the army would remain loyal. Prats avoided the question, reminding Allende that in 1891 when the army had stayed loyal it had caused civil war and much bloodshed. Prats did not want any blood on his conscience and he refused to take sides.[27] Pinochet had no such qualms. Just over a year later Prats was killed in Buenos Aires by a bomb planted on his car.

Just before 9 a.m., Isabel, Allende's youngest daughter arrived at La Moneda. Allende begged both his daughters to leave. The Junta demanded immediate surrender. Allende refused. At 9.03 a.m. he again addressed the nation this time via Magallanes Radio, a communist party station, and the last remaining on air. 'The planes are passing overhead. It is possible they will gun us down. But let them know that we are here, at least with our example they will see that in this country there are men that know how to fulfil their obligations.' He repeated his condemnation of the generals and expressed an unshakeable optimism in the future,

In the name of the most sacred interest of the people, and in the name of the fatherland, I call on you to say have faith. History cannot be stopped by either repression or crime. This is a stage that will be overcome. This is a hard and difficult moment, it is possible that we will be crushed, but tomorrow belongs to the people, belongs to the workers.

Conscious of the imminence of defeat he urged the people 'to be alert and vigilant. It should not allow itself to be provoked, nor massacred, but it should also defend its conquests. It should defend the right to build a better and more dignified life by its own efforts.'

He then organised the defence of the building, posting defenders at the windows of the upper floor. Six regiments with tanks surrounded the Moneda. Allende's final battle would take place here, sandwiched between the US Embassy on Constitution Square, and the US military group stationed in the Ministry of Defence. The Moneda's defenders fired from the windows and from some of the surrounding buildings. There were less than 60 of them. Another message was received from the generals – immediate surrender and Allende to go over to the Ministry of Defence. Allende responded, 'A president of Chile does not surrender, and he receives people in the Moneda. If Pinochet wants me to go to the ministry, tell him not to be such a coward, and that he should come and get me personally!' Allende then told the palace police guard that they could leave. An emissary from the Socialist Party leadership, which had so often proclaimed the inevitability of violence, arrived wanting to find out what the situation was and asking Allende to move to a defensible position. Allende bitterly replied, 'I'll fulfil my duty here, let the party fulfil its own.'[28]

At 9.15 a.m. Allende gave his last speech to the people of Chile. Most of the defenders gathered to hear it. Allende held the phone communicating him to Radio Magallanes in one hand and his AKM in the other. A military helmet sat atop his head and contrasted with his tweed jacket and turtleneck jumper. This last speech was an emotive farewell. He called Radio Magallanes, the phone was lifted up at the other end. 'Who's speaking?' 'Ravest, comrade.' 'Comrade I need you to get me on air immediately.' For days he had known that his time was coming. In his speeches he had repeatedly made it clear that 'only by riddling me with bullets will they get me to leave the Moneda.' Nine days before he had told his Colombian lover, Gloria Gaitan, that 'I am a man who has but two hours of life left, a week, or maybe a month...'. On that 11 September, Allende was a man who knew he was living his last hours. The radio crew barely had time to play a few bars of the national anthem before putting him on air while they scrambled to record what Allende would say, forgetting to switch off their own microphones: 'This is probably the last opportunity for me to speak to you.' Allende began.

The air force has bombed the towers of Radio Portales and Radio Corporacion. My words contain no bitterness, just disappointment. May they be a moral punishment for those who have betrayed the oaths they took: the soldiers of Chile, the titular commanders-in-chief, Admiral Merino, who has designated himself the commander of the Navy, and Mr Mendoza, that despicable general who only yesterday was declaring his fidelity and loyalty to the Government, and who has also designated himself Director-General of Carabineros. Faced with these actions the only thing I can say to the traitors is "I will not resign!"

Placed in a historic moment, I will repay the loyalty of the people with my life. And I say to you that I have the certainty that the seed that we have sown in the dignified conscience of thousands and thousands of Chileans cannot be destroyed definitively. They have the force, they may overcome us, but social processes cannot be stopped, neither by crimes nor with force. History is ours and peoples make it.

Workers of my fatherland, I want to thank you for the loyalty that you have always shown, the trust that you deposited in a man who was just an interpreter of your great desires for justice, who gave his word that the Constitution and the Law would be respected, and who did so. In this defining moment, the last in which I can address you, I want you to learn the lesson: foreign capital and imperialism, united with the reaction, created the climate for the armed forces to break their tradition that was taught to them by General Schneider and reaffirmed by Commander Araya, victims of the same social sector that today is in its houses, waiting for power to be reconquered by the hands of others, in order to continue defending their profits and their privileges.

I address myself above all to the modest woman of our land, the peasant who believed in us, the worker who worked harder, the mother who understood our concern for the children. I address the professionals of the fatherland, the patriotic professionals who continued to work against the sedition supported by the professional organisations, those class organisations that defended the advantages given to them by a capitalist society.

I address the youth, those who sang and gave your joy and your spirit of struggle. I address the man of Chile, the worker, the peasant, the intellectual, those who will be persecuted, because fascism has been present in our country for many hours now – in the terrorist attacks, blowing up bridges, cutting railway lines, destroying oil and gas pipelines right before the eyes of those who had the duty to act. They too were committed. History will judge them.

Radio Magallanes will surely be silenced, and the calm tones of my voice will no longer reach you. It doesn't matter. You will continue to hear me. I will always be with you. At least the memory of me will be of a dignified man who was loyal to the fatherland.

The people should defend themselves, without sacrificing themselves. The people should not allow themselves to be devastated, nor gunned down. Nor can they allow themselves to be humiliated.

Workers of my fatherland, I have faith in Chile and in its destiny. Other men will overcome this grey and bitter moment when treachery tries to impose itself. Go on knowing that, much sooner than later the great avenues upon which the free man walks in order to build a better society will open up again.

Viva Chile! Viva the People! Long live the workers!

These are my last words and I am certain that my sacrifice will not be in vain, I am certain that at least, it will be a moral lesson that will punish felony cowardice and treachery.

His remaining followers, about 40 people, including his daughters and his lover and secretary Mireya 'Payita' Contreras, stood in choked silence as he finished. He replaced the telephone receiver. Tears were flowing down many cheeks. Some of his closest collaborators, his daughters and his friends embraced him.

Allende released anyone in state service. He gathered his three military aides, and told them 'Tell your commanders that I'm not leaving here and I will not surrender. That if they want me to resign that they come and ask me to do it themselves. They should have the courage to do it personally. They won't get me out of here even if they do bomb us.' Allende told them that his last bullet would be saved for himself 'like this', and he gestured, jabbing his fingers upwards under his chin. The aides left, taking the military cooks, and the Carabineros palace guard with them. The civilian detectives stayed. Next, Allende tried to convince the women to leave, and he finally managed to get his daughters to go, inventing a message for Fidel Castro. Once outside Beatriz repented, and frantically knocked on the door to be allowed back in. Nobody opened and Isabel dragged her away to shelter. Payita had hidden from Allende and remained in the palace until the end. Then Allende sent away all those who did not know how to shoot. Joan Garcés, the Spanish social scientist who had tried to theorise Allendismo, was sent away along with ministers and other collaborators 'You must tell the world about our government and what has happened here today', Allende insisted. The air force Hawker Hunter jets arrived in the skies above the city. The wife of the US ambassador, Nathaniel Davis, described their flight as they fired their missiles at the Presidential Palace: 'It was an eerily beautiful sight as they came in from nowhere. The sun glinted on their wings.' The first rockets hit the front of the palace, blasting through the thick walls. The explosions were deafening and the defenders sheltered from the blasts and the fire. Allende covered Payita's body with his own. He had told her that the military would not dare bombard the Moneda. 'Looks like they did dare after all' he joked to her as they lay amid the dust and smoke. The next aircraft fired its rockets down through the roof, setting the building ablaze. The fires began to spread. The police fired tear gas into the inferno from circling helicopters. The defenders choked on the fumes. The shooting was incessant. Allende fired from the windows of his offices over Constitution Square, almost diagonally opposite the US Embassy. Smoke billowed from the windows, and the national flag burned on its pole above the main entrance.

At the Moneda the attack continued. Tanks tried to force the main doors. Allende and a GAP bodyguard fired RPGs at them, forcing them back. GAP members posted in nearby buildings covered the approaches to the palace. Allende ordered someone to call the Tomas Moro residence. A bodyguard answered and informed them that the house has also been rocketed by aircraft, destroying much of it. One aircraft missed its target, hitting the air force hospital next door. Tencha hid under a desk while the house disintegrated around her. Allende's face creased in pain. He headed upstairs where he fired at the attackers from the balcony of this private secretary's office.[29] Escorted by members of the GAP Tencha escaped to a friend's house. The bodyguards then tried to reach the Moneda. The house was later ransacked by the army and by neighbours, paintings and the library stolen or destroyed. As with so much else looted from UP supporters after the coup, most items have never been returned or found.

In the centre, ministry functionaries cowered in basements or in the inner rooms of the solid buildings. Gloria Gaitan was in one when the planes attacked the Moneda 'Finally, they've killed that son of a whore!' shouted one woman. Gaitan dashed over and shook her by the throat before being dragged away in tears by her friends. In the wealthy neighbourhoods some people began hanging out Chilean flags in celebration. In the Moneda Allende still fired from his exposed position on the balcony. One of the doctors in the building grabbed him by the feet and dragged him back inside. 'Let me go, *huevon*!' shouted Allende, before turning and saying, 'Oh, it's you Jironcito.'[30]

Soon afterwards one of the defenders, Augusto '*Perro*' Olivares, Allende's close friend and the head of National Television, committed suicide. It was a harsh blow to morale. Allende asked the defenders for a minute's silence in his honour and then ordered four of the defenders out to negotiate a truce with the attackers, probably in the hope of saving their lives. At one point he ordered the GAP to 'Knock down all those shitty old men', referring to the plaster busts of Chile's past presidents, 'except for Balmaceda and Pedro Aguirre Cerda.' The busts were smashed and the floor of the halls littered with broken plaster. The attack began again, the air thick with bullets, explosions, smoke, dust and tear gas.

With ammunition running low and the defenders exhausted, alone, isolated and without hope of relief, Allende called them together and ordered them to surrender. The GAP in the buildings covering the Moneda had also run out of ammunition and began their escape from the centre. As the defenders discussed surrender, troops smashed their way in through the Moneda's

side door, known as Morande 80. Shots rang out and boots
could be heard crunching on the debris downstairs. One of the
several doctors in the Moneda, Oscar Soto, bumped into the
advancing troops on the stairs. An officer saved him from being
shot and sent him upstairs to negotiate the surrender. Allende
ordered all the defenders out, 'all of you, go downstairs, leave
your weapons, don't leave anything in your pockets. Leave with
dignity, surrender because this is a massacre.'[31] Allende said he
would be the last to leave. The defenders organised themselves
in a line. Payita was put first, wearing Augusto Olivares' jacket,
with Chile's Declaration of Independence hidden in one sleeve. As
they began to descend, Allende suddenly stepped from towards
the back of the line, opened the door of the Independence Salon,
and closed it behind him. Two men heard him shout, 'Allende
doesn't surrender, dammit!' The men in the line were confused.
'Where's he going?' asked Dr Arturo Jiron, 'To commit suicide',
answered Dr Ruiz. Downstairs boots and rifle butts were used to
hurry the defenders outside, where they were forced down onto
the ground, hands on their heads. Payita had Olivares' jacket
torn off her shoulders, a soldier ripped up the Declaration of
Independence that fell out.

Upstairs, 'Jano', one of the GAP defenders opened the door
Allende had closed behind himself. The others crowded around
him. Through the smoke and dust they saw Allende sitting facing
them on a red sofa, wreathed in smoke, diffuse light pouring in
from two large windows either side of him. Behind him a large
painting of the proclamation of independence hung on the wall.
Allende saw their faces and shouted, 'Shut the door!' Before any
other them could react, President Allende seemed to rise off the
sofa, his face becoming smudged, as if dissolving in the smoke.
The men heard a shot. Dr 'Pachi' Guijon rushed in and took
Allende's pulse. He was dead. 'What do I do now?' he thought
to himself. Allende's wristwatch continued to tick. Others stood
by the door observing the scene. One of them burst into tears,
they turned and began to descend the staircase leading out of the
burning palace. Dr Guijon remained by Allende's side. On the
staircase Enrique Huerta, one of the defenders, shouted out 'The
President has died! Viva Allende! Don't surrender comrades!'

But others grabbed his gun. They did not know that torture and disappearance lay ahead of them.[32]

Dr Guijon remained by Allende's side for ten minutes or so, sitting on a small stool. Realising that he was too near Allende's AKM, he moved it a little further away, across the President's body. Two soldiers entered, Dr Guijon raised his hands. Firemen followed the soldiers, and behind them came General Palacios, the man in charge of the operation to take the palace. He observed the scene. Allende lay back over the red sofa, his assault rifle across his lap. His hands were blackened with gunpowder. His face was hardly recognisable; the top of his head was missing. Palacios then radioed out to Admiral Carvajal. 'Mission accomplished. The Moneda is taken. The President is dead.' Carvajal in turn immediately informed the Junta, in English – 'They say that Allende committed suicide and is dead now.' Then in Spanish 'tell me if you understood.'

8
What Followed Allende?

Allende's death marked the beginning of a dark period in Chilean history. The military treated Chile like an occupied country. Football stadiums, and army barracks became detention centres. Hundreds of thousands of people were arrested and detained over the next few months. Foreigners were particularly sought out as members of a supposed guerrilla army that had been assembled under Allende. Soldiers disobeying orders were shot, senior officers perceived as close to Allende were arrested and tortured, and some were killed. The ordinary members of Chile's left wing parties and trade unions were hunted down and many were killed and disappeared. Dozens of children were killed or tortured. Thousands were abandoned to their fate as parents disappeared into torture camps and prisons. In the countryside landowners took a violent revenge on peasants and the Mapuche indigenous people. Hundreds of thousands of Chileans were forced into exile. Allende had feared civil war, but in the end Chile was subjected to a massacre. The left's strength in numbers was simply swept aside by violence.

On 18 September Eduardo Frei went to the newly installed Junta's Independence Day blessing in Santiago Cathedral. His presence as President of the Senate, alongside two other former Presidents was a powerful legitimation of the new regime. In October Patricio Aylwin the president of the PDC met with the military junta. Although what happened is disputed, events appear to support the version that asserts that Aylwin endorsed the coup and offered the cooperation of PDC members on an individual basis in the hope that power might yet be handed to him.[1] Other leading Christian Democrats such as Radimiro Tomic and Bernardo Leighton immediately condemned the coup. The National Party dissolved itself. The Junta dissolved Congress.

Figure 8.1 The Moneda palace the day after the bombings, 12 September 1973. Credit: Naul Ojeda.

While the priests incanted their blessing, Chile's democracy was being sacrificed along with the lives of thousands of anonymous people who had hoped for a better future.

Pinochet gradually consolidated his rule and began implementing a project intended to extirpate 'the Marxist cancer' from Chile. The education system was purged of leftists and military officers placed in charge. Public figures that might have unified the opposition in exile were assassinated, with General Prats murdered in Buenos Aires in October 1974, PDC leader Bernardo Leighton shot and crippled in Rome in 1975, and former Chilean ambassador to the US Orlando Letelier murdered in a Washington car-bombing in September 1976. In 1982 Eduardo Frei, who had done so much to prevent a political agreement with Allende, was poisoned and killed after he threatened to unite the opposition to the dictatorship. It is symbolic that the military murdered both presidents that had striven to reform Chile, one within capitalism and the other through socialism.

In 1977 Pinochet laid the basis for a new constitution in a speech to a nocturnal congregation bearing burning torches.[2] Three years later it was enshrined after a military-controlled plebiscite. The 1980 constitution, although reformed, still forms the basis of the Chilean constitution to this day. Its eighth article outlawed Marxism. It made Pinochet president and guaranteed his rule to 1990, with the possibility of extending it to 1997. It enshrined a 'binomial' electoral system which severely distorts the electoral process, and a Labour Code that severely weakened labour organisation, and it re-privatised part of the copper mining industry, and opened up other mining sectors to foreign companies. It also enshrined the private ownership of underground resources. The dictatorship lowered import tariffs, prompting a flood of imports and the closure of most of Chile's industry. Unemployment and poverty shot up and wages collapsed, rolling back decades of social progress.

The Christian Democrats moved into the opposition, but despite myriad communist concessions, the PDC leadership still refused to ally with them. Time passed and frustrations grew. Inside Chile the left began to organise to strike back. The MIR tried to install a guerrilla movement, but it was destroyed. The Socialist Party split. The 1982 debt crisis sparked mass resistance to the regime, and a year later the Communists launched a 'Manuel Rodríguez Patriotic Front' aimed at defending the mobilisations and building towards a 'National Uprising'. In September 1986 Pinochet narrowly survived the ambush of his cavalcade, and amid growing fears of a revolutionary overthrow in both Washington and Santiago the Reagan administration made strenuous efforts to identify and support 'moderate' sectors in the regime and among the opposition who would be amenable to an alliance excluding the Communist Party. The Catholic Church was recruited to the cause, alongside an array of foreign NGOs who worked hard to promote a transition to democracy.

With this amenable opposition guaranteed, the regime began to implement a transition towards 'democracy' after 1986. The steady collapse of 'existing socialism' in Europe formed a potent backdrop that sucked strength from the left. Eventually under US pressure the 'moderate' Socialist and Christian Democrat opposition accepted Pinochet's 1980 constitution while US support of moderates in the military encouraged engagement. But the democracy born of the transition was a mutation that served to preserve an unjust economic system. On the cusp of the handover of power in 1990 Pinochet added several articles to his constitution that ensured his control over the incoming civilian government. These included the creation of 'designated senators' and decentralising and privatising education. Pinochet retired and then appointed a new supreme court, he ensured congress had no remit to investigate members of the 'military regime'. With everything in place the civilian *Concertacion* government took power, a new alliance of Christian Democrats and 'renovated' socialists.

Over the next 20 years the Concertacion ruled Chile, implementing a sort of underdeveloped social democracy through coalition. Among its first measures was the demobilisation of the vast popular movement that had sprung up in resistance to the dictatorship. The Concertacion tried to diversify Chilean exports, and agro-industry, fishing, fruits and wood became important sectors. The economy continued to grow, but it was recovering from a very low base. Foreign investment flooded in, money from copper and mining flowed out. Chile remained dependent on raw material exports. What growth was achieved was unevenly distributed. Instead of redistribution by taxation and wage increases, the Concertacion used income from copper mining to target extreme poverty. Inequality remained embedded in the system. With the left largely excluded from the system thanks to an ideological crisis and the intricacies of the binomial system, and the trade unions crippled by a repressive Labour Code and a 'flexible' workforce, only in 2000 did average wages achieve their 1970 levels. Chile remained overwhelmingly dependent on what Allende had called 'the wage of Chile' – copper. The Concertacion also failed to rigorously pursue human rights abusers, and it was not until Pinochet's arrest in London in 1997 that the curtain of impunity began to be lifted on any but the most notorious abusers. The civilian faces behind the military remained untouched. Popular discontent bubbled away, but it was held in check by the potent combination of a steady improvement in people's economic situation, the introduction of easily available credit and a latent fear of a return to military rule. Together, credit cards, television, internet, mobile phones and the accoutrements of modernisation encouraged an 'I don't care' attitude.

In 2010, with discontent with the Concertacion mounting, the centrist coalition put forward an unpopular candidate, Eduardo Frei junior. The result was that Sebastian Piñera, the billionaire brother of one of Pinochet's Interior Ministers, became president of Chile. Dozens of Pinochet supporters, among them notorious human rights abusers, stepped out of the shadows and back into the political limelight. The right saw it as a popular vindication, but during the same elections the Communist Party finally managed to win four congressional seats. The Concertacion suffered its first desertions, and the Socialist Party began to fracture. Chilean politics had in fact begun to polarise again.

Under Piñera Chile has witnessed the largest demonstrations since the dictatorship, with Santiago and other cities seeing the return of the famous '*cacerolazos*' of the 1980s, when the urban population would take advantage of blackouts to beat pots and pans and beep car horns to demonstrate their discontent. In 2011 students mobilised demanding that education be properly funded, and in effect renationalised. Organised workers have also been on strike, alongside mobilisations by environmental activists and indigenous people. They have been heavily repressed. As in the 1920s, a new generation of trade unionists, student leaders and political activists is shaking the foundations of Chile's political structure. Today the post-coup institutionality is creaking under pressure from the masses and there are signs that 'Allendismo' is once more inspiring Chile's youth, from the nationalisation of copper, to the provision of quality health and education, and indigenous rights. Chileans are again demanding sovereignty and democracy. This is the essence of Allende's legacy.

9
Life and Legacy

Salvador Allende died at the age of 65. By his own admission he had lived a relatively long and fruitful life. It was a life dedicated to the struggle for democracy and a life defined by elections often contested in difficult circumstances. Allende's persistence in fighting elections was testament to his belief that in Chile, because of its unique history and social context, this was the most viable and effective way of placing the country on the path to socialism.

Allende's conviction was not a wilful construct. He was born during the dying stages of the post-1891 system, and he became an adult as the democratic system that lasted until 11 September 1973 was born. As the scion of a family with a distinguished history, Allende had lived a privileged childhood amid members of the Chilean political elite. As a student Allende had mixed with many future political leaders and was witness to the growth and development of the popular organisations of the left. As a young adult he also witnessed the failure of the military-inspired 'socialist republic' of 1932, contrasted in 1938 by the successful election of a Popular Front government that began a process of radical reforms. All helped to shape his perception that, in Chile the revolution did not have to follow the 'traditional' violent path. Allende decided to act 'in accordance with the reality of my country, in conformity with its idiosyncrasies and needs', as he later said.[1] His concrete, practical and intimate knowledge of the political system convinced him that in Chile it was possible to initiate deep structural change from within.

Learning from the experience of the Popular Front, Allende thought that this approach required the broadest possible coalition of people and organisations around proposals that aimed at achieving democracy, social justice and economic and human development. The Communist Party came to a similar conclusion. Fortunately for both, much of the Socialist Party, while sceptical of a multi-class alliance, was amenable to a narrow alliance of working class organisations. However, for much of the 1940s and 1950s the Socialist Party was itself divided. This was reflected in the division of the trade union movement as well. Allende played an important role in rebuilding socialist unity, and once this was achieved, in sustaining the alliance with the Communist Party that took him to the Presidency after 18 years of struggle.

Allende was one of the left's best known and most respected leaders among a generation of political stars forged during the Popular Front. Together they helped to shape the Chilean left – one of the most vibrant, best organised and most effective in the world. Allende was without doubt the figure that stood tallest among them, thanks to his knowledge of the system, his work rate, combativeness, and his deep compassion for the people, his capacity to educate and to gather bright minds around him, along with a public persona shaped over decades of public life. In addition Allende had an ability to think tactically and strategically, to grasp the essence of a situation rapidly and to look further forward than those around him. This showed the influence of a particular set of political ideas and guiding principles. While it is true that Allende did not develop a universal political theory it would be a mistake not to recognise a particular 'Allendista' set of principles. He had what Regis Debray called 'a firm conceptual foundation.' He read widely, especially about politics, and although he may not have read many of the more recent Marxist theoreticians, he had no doubt learned much about them from his conversations with those that had. His intellectual legacy is in this sense a mixture of concepts drawn from a broad spectrum of sources and life experiences. In this he was truly a 'heterodox' thinker. It was Allende's political vision, along with his fearlessness, his charisma, his international contacts, his national stature and his total dedication to the cause that made him the irreplaceable leader of the Chilean left.

Allende spent his life in the search for the unity of the
left, without compromising its diversity. He did not seek the
construction of a narrow vanguard, but the development of a
mass movement. This movement would seek points of agreement
with the political centre, while maintaining a firm commitment
to anti-imperialism and to socialism. Allende's Popular Unity
government was the culmination of this 50-year effort to build
the broadest possible coalition. In election campaign after
election campaign Allende, the CUT trade union federation
and the parties of the left sought to spread their analysis of
Chile's problems and their solutions to the people, evolving and
adapting their programme as they went. Gradually, and against
the odds they convinced a majority of Chileans. The growth of
the left's influence dragged the entire political spectrum leftwards
to such an extent that the PDC, its main competition, aped its
programme and its language.

The Popular Unity was the culmination of Allende's efforts
to forge a broad coalition. But just as the Popular Unity was
the triumph of his methods and his message, as President of
the country Allende also bears some responsibility for the
ultimate failure of the Popular Unity. There are a variety of
explanations usually given for this defeat. Those critical from
the left have tended to emphasize his underestimation of the
threat from the United States, and the inevitability of the failure
of an unarmed revolution. Other radical critiques focus on his
unwillingness to arm the people, or mobilise them in defence
of the process, and upon the government's failure to support
incipient political organisations that began to form outside the
traditional institutions. The Communist critique centred on the
failure to deal with the 'ultraleft' within and outside the UP
coalition, and on Allende's failure to use coercion against the
more extreme right-wing opposition, which together resulted
in the 'isolation of the working class'. Liberal critiques have in
turn emphasized that economic chaos and political polarisation,
along with the structural restrictions of the political system
created an unworkable situation, and that Allende's failure to
retreat from his revolutionary goals therefore made the coup
inevitable. Perhaps each of these rather general explanations

contains some truth at particular points during the Popular Unity. None, however, explains why Allende acted as he did. To find the answer we must look into the mind of the man who led the process, and who therefore had the greatest potential to change the course of events.

Key to understanding Allende's actions is understanding what he meant by 'revolution'. Some have argued that Allende was a reformist who became a revolutionary in later years. However, Allende always sought to transform Chilean society and do away with capitalism. Those who accused him of being a social-democrat mistakenly confused the methods of his struggle with the desired outcome. Allende did not want to destroy his opponents, but to liberate them. Allende wanted to build on the solid foundations of the past, not upon its smoking ruins. Allende sought to avoid the social costs of other revolutionary processes, and he tried to maintain Chile's social cohesion, but he did not want to preserve capitalism. Allende aimed at creating the conditions for a transition away from dependent capitalism towards independent, sovereign and democratic socialism. Crucially, Allende saw Latin America's underdevelopment as the result of the combination between exploitative upper classes and their subordination of the region to the United States. Internationally, it was vital that Chile throw off US domination because it distorted politics, crippled the economy, and severely limited Chile's international relations. It was therefore vital that Chile develop good relations with other countries seeking a similar independence, and with those of the socialist world. This struggle was not just in Chile's interests – it was necessary to end exploitation and inequality internationally because this would liberate the exploiters from their 'sentence of despotism.' Therefore the failure of Latin American nationalists like Romulo Betancourt was due to their failure to challenge the basis of elite power and imperialism.[2] For Allende, socialism was true nationalism, and the solution to Chile's problems required linked national and international action. This was what shaped Allende's thinking and prevented him from being another reformist nationalist.

For Allende socialism was both a strategy of socio-economic development and a means to achieve human fulfilment. It was a way to make real the promise of the slogan 'liberty, equality and fraternity' which inspired the Latin American independence struggles. Under the influence of these ideas Allende's socialism had to include tolerance of diversity within the left, and tolerance of the opposition. The way to combine this with a revolutionary transformation of state and society was through participatory democracy, since through it pluralism of opinion and thus true liberty could be achieved. But in order for democracy to function effectively also required social justice. Democracy and socialism were therefore two halves of the same coin. This concern with democracy and the realities of the Chilean political system translated into an almost obsessive search for the support of the majority and a rejection of the coercive role of the state.

In order to achieve social justice it was vital to provide preventative healthcare, quality education, and decent living conditions for all Chileans, to end the hidden violence caused by malnutrition, ill health and poor housing. Development had to be funded by public control of Chile's natural resources, and by a programme of agrarian reform and industrialisation that would give the state a principal role in the economy. However, it was not enough simply to enable the state to play a major role. The very purpose of the state needed to be transformed to serve the interests of ordinary working people. Yes, the state had been created by the oligarchy, but it could act against it if enough 'social force' could be applied. Allende thus understood the state to have some autonomy from its origins as an instrument of the ruling class.[3] The subsequent economic development would provide the resources to achieve the 'most noble potential' of each, and allow Chileans to 'join civilisation' as masters of their destiny. Economic development and state control of resources were thus a precondition for the creation of socialism. In a similar way Allende saw the existing legal system as an incomplete conquest by the people. Therefore this legal system based on liberalism could, and needed to be *transformed* into a more advanced socialist form, not completely destroyed.

Allende's socialism was democratic and undogmatic, he spoke of the need to develop the theories and the practice of the new forms of organisation that would develop, he did not already have a clear vision of what would happen and how, rather his government would begin to provide the spaces in which these new forms would develop democratically. This approach also envisioned the long period of time necessary for people, if necessary over generations, to adjust to socialist ethics and values. Therefore the gradual reformism of the Chilean road was also the way to guarantee socialism. Together, anti-imperialism, participatory democracy, pluralism and the transformation of the state made Allende's road revolutionary. These concepts explain why Allende rejected the use of force during the Popular Unity, since violence would itself alter the kind of socialism being built. Unfortunately for Allende, and for the Popular Unity, the global context of the 1960s and 1970s created an environment where many came to fetishize violence and dogmatic ideas about the seizure of power. As a result, Allende's road was misunderstood by many who otherwise shared his goals.

After so many years in opposition, when Allende won the 1970 elections he knew that his government would face strong opposition from the Chilean elite, as well as from the US government. The example of US pressure and interference on Chilean governments and society since the late 1940s, the US interventions against Guatemala and Cuba, all served to make Allende aware of the probability of such an intervention against his government. Furthermore, he was familiar with the Marxist observation that each revolution provoked a counter-revolution, often with foreign support. Allende's government also received multiple warnings of the Nixon administration's hostility towards the Popular Unity. Therefore Allende was not naïve about the probability of US hostility. In fact the construction of a broad alliance for change was both a method to achieve democratic socialism, and a way of ensuring the security of the process in the face of US hostility.

Therefore Allende's political strategy depended upon the construction of a solid social and political majority with the support of the Christian Democrat grassroots, and that of its parliamentary representatives. The only way for the UP project to succeed was to continue bringing more and more people together in support of the goals of the revolution, turning the national majority for change into a political majority within Congress. The problem was thus Allende's main area of concern, and he sought to bring together the two political movements that argued for a transformation towards socialism in Chile – the 'popular movement' embodied in the UP and those within the PDC who supported the ideals of 'communitarian socialism' and much of the UP programme. Only then could the legislative framework for the socio-economic changes necessary be created. This explains Allende's unwavering commitment to a policy of alliances with the centre. The problem was that his own coalition was not fully behind him in this.

Allende doggedly sought to create an alliance with the PDC throughout his time in office. At first he sought such an alliance in Congress, seeking to force the PDC to make good its leftist and nationalist rhetoric by becoming co-sponsors of a package of reforms nationalising copper and simultaneously creating the mechanisms for institutional change. Unfortunately Allende's efforts were stymied by resistance and incomprehension within both the UP and the PDC.[4] The referendum package idea sank when the UP leadership preferred to separate the economic and political reforms being proposed. The UP thus failed to consolidate its victory and eventually allowed the opposition to take the initiative. However, Allende never stopped trying to achieve a deal.

It is testament to Allende's vision that this strategy came close to success on several occasions. Among those that share responsibility for its ultimate failure are those leaders of the PDC who preferred to help destroy Chile's democratic system rather than allow Allende's process to continue. To a lesser extent the extremist leaders of the PS and other groups who sought a confrontation, and the military officers whose loyalty to the constitution did not stretch to defending it also bear some responsibility. But the greatest responsibility lies with the US government, since without the US intervention not only was the Chilean elite too small and too weak to hold back Allende and the UP's revolutionary process, but it is highly likely that the PDC would have eventually allied with the UP. US intervention did much to remove the incentives for this alliance, and it did much to finance and link together the forces of opposition. Yet, even with this intervention it took three years of sabotage to break Chile's institutionality, destroy its democratic traditions, and undermine the constitutionalists within the Chilean armed forces.

Today it is the internal contradictions of the post coup model that are weakening Chile's institutionality. It is no accident that the Allende's legacy is gathering interest at the same time as capitalism endures its most serious crisis since the collapse of the Soviet Union. During the years that socialism was seen as a pipe dream, Allende's legacy could be brushed under the carpet as a relic from a bygone age. Today however, it is becoming increasingly clear that Chile and the world need an alternative to neoliberalism and the failures of social democracy. At the same time in the rest of Latin America left-wing governments are developing processes bearing striking similarities to the Popular Unity. In this context people are beginning to look back at Allende's ideas in search of guidance.

The idea of the need for public control of natural resources is again becoming widespread in Chile as people search for ways to fund the improvements to education and public services. At the same time many are criticising high levels of inequality, arguing for a fairer distribution of wealth. Interestingly, the mass mobilisations of recent years have shown a remarkable similarity with those of the early twentieth century. While many within the social movements question the need for broad alliances, or participation in what they argue is an illegitimate system, it is likely that the future will see movements and parties coming together to change the most pernicious aspects of Pinochet's legacy. It is also likely that initially, as in the 1930s and 1940s, these alliances will not be led by the left, but by the centre, and just as likely that as before, the left in some new form will come to dominate again since, as Allende argued, social democracy cannot resolve the problems of countries in the 'over-exploited' world. While it may take time, political experience will show that the path chosen by Recabarren and by Allende, that of building unity, and struggling both within and outside the institutions of the political system is the most effective way of achieving profound and lasting social change.

One of the reasons for optimism is the example being shown by the left in other parts of Latin America. While Chile remains somewhat insulated from changes in Argentina, Bolivia, Ecuador and Venezuela, it cannot remain so forever. Already Chileans are looking to these countries, as well as Brazil, for inspiration. It is interesting to note that processes with goals and methods remarkably similar to Allende's are in development in much of Latin America. They share a heavy emphasis on Latin American and Third World solidarity, a lack of dogmatic ideological solutions, an acknowledgement of the importance of the state in the economy, and an emphasis on democracy, pluralism and participation in both economy and politics. These progressive processes in Venezuela and elsewhere have all come to power through elections. In each of them the development of supportive mass movements was crucial to victory, as has been the educating role of the principal leaders, people such as Rafael Correa, Hugo Chavez, Cristina Fernandez and Evo Morales.

In the wake of Allende's overthrow, the left in Latin America and throughout the world sought to draw lessons from defeat. Allende's defeat was a concrete lesson in the methods that imperialism would use against any leftist process. However, the left also remained inspired by Chile's democratic socialism. On the one hand Chile proved that the electoral road was viable, and on the other, it highlighted the need to effectively defend the revolutionary process. Each of today's leftist processes has faced stiff internal opposition and some form of hostility from the United States. In Honduras and Paraguay the opposition has even triumphed. However, in general the new generation of progressive governments have demonstrated an appreciation both of the importance of what they call 'military patriots' in their survival, as is most notable in Venezuela, and of the importance of popular mobilisation in defence of the revolution. Unlike in Chile, in the modern processes the revolutionaries have sought to create new mechanisms of popular power at the same time as they transform the structures and the purpose of the state. Therefore these processes are, as Chavez said 'peaceful, but not unarmed.'[5]

The search by Latin America's new left for an independent and non-aligned foreign policy, and for the political and economic integration of Latin America, also echo Allende's policies, and in all of this Allende is recognised and hailed as their precursor. Allende is thus more recognised abroad, where politicians seek to implement his methods, and where schools, streets and squares are named after him, than he is at home where a solitary statue stands outside the Moneda palace.

However, the recent mobilisations in Chile promise an awakening from the long night following September 1973. Perhaps soon, as Allende predicted on that grim September morning, 'the great avenues' that Chileans will walk in order to build a better society will open up again. In order to do so Chileans will need to build upon the legacy left them by Salvador Allende and the Popular Unity.

Notes

CHAPTER 1

1. Frei to Allende, quoted by Valdes in Gabriel Valdes, *Sueños y memorias* (Santiago: Taurus, 2009), p. 210.
2. Kissinger speaking to Gabriel Valdes, Chilean foreign minister, June 1969.
3. Speech to the students of the University of Concepcion, 4 May 1972.
4. Brian Loveman, *Chile: The Legacy of Hispanic Capitalism*, (New York: OUP, 1988), p. 42.
5. Alberto Cabero, 'El roto', in *El caracter chileno*, ed. Hernán Godoy Urzua (Santiago: Editorial Universitaria, 1991), p. 380.
6. Loveman, p. 43.
7. Tomas Lago 'Asi es el huaso' in *El caracter chileno*, p. 390.
8. See Maurice Zeitlin, *The Civil Wars in Chile*, (Princeton: Princeton University Press, 1984); Hernán Ramírez Necochea, *Balmaceda y la contrarrevolucion de 1891*, (Santiago: Editorial Universitaria, 1958).
9. Edwin Williamson, *The Penguin History of Latin America*, (London: Penguin, 1998), p. 485.
10. Loveman, p. 208.
11. Luis Sicilia, *Luis Emilio Recabarren*, (Buenos Aires: Capital Intellectual, 2007), p. 33.
12. Loveman, p. 194.

CHAPTER 2

1. In Hispanic cultures the paternal surname precedes the maternal one, but both are retained. There is some debate as to whether Allende was in fact born in Santiago since a birth certificate asserting this has been unearthed. However, Allende always spoke of himself as a citizen of Valparaiso, and moreover, it was common at the time not to register children immediately, and it may be that Allende was registered in Santiago after actually having been born in Valparaiso.
2. The liberators of Latin America organised themselves in the Lautaro Lodge to fight for independence. This then developed into the Chilean freemasonry, which therefore had close links with enlightenment ideas and the struggle for independence.
3. Regis Debray, *Conversations with Allende. Socialism in Chile* (London: NLB, 1971), p. 66.
4. The British nitrate magnate John Thomas North contributed £100,000 to the rebellion. The rebels' victory made him fantastically rich. British ships also provided coal and other supplies to the rebel forces.

5. Ramirez Necochea, pp. 214–16.
6. Fredy Gambetta recounts this story in Eduardo Labarca, *Salvador Allende: biografía sentimental* (Santiago: Catalonia, 2007), pp. 30–1.
7. Fernando Alegria, *Allende. Mi vecino el presidente.* (Santiago: Planeta, 1989).
8. Gloria Gaitan, *El compañero presidente* (Bogota: Margen Izquierdo, 1973) p. 88.
9. Alegria, p. 45.
10. Miguel Labarca, *Allende en persona: Testimonio de una intensa Amistad y colaboración,* (Santiago: Ediciones Chile América, 2008), p. 31.
11. Chilean newspapers of the day. *El Mercurio* remains a bastion of conservatism.
12. Cited in Jorge Arrate and Eduardo Rojas, *Memoria de la izquierda chilena* (Santiago: Grupo Zeta, 2003), vol. 1, p. 110.
13. M. Labarca, pp. 31, 35.
14. Miguel's son, Eduardo, later wrote an excellent biography of Allende.
15. Diana Veneros, *Allende: Un ensayo psicobiografico* (Santiago: Señales, 2003), p. 44.
16. It should be remembered that only 4 or 5 per cent of the population could vote at this time.
17. Julio Cesar Jobet, *Historia del Partido Socialista de Chile* (Santiago: Ediciones Documentas, 1987), p. 30.
18. Iosef Lavretsky, *Salvador Allende* (Moscow: Molodaya Gvardiya, 1974), p. 28.
19. Regis Debray, *Conversations with Allende. Socialism in Chile* (London: NLB, 1971), p. 64.
20. Oscar Waiss, *Chile vivo: memorias de un socialista,* (Madrid: CESA, 1986), p. 24.
21. Ibid., p. 21.
22. Jorquera, p. 47.
23. The minister, Pedro Blanquier, declared that the government had 5 million pesos left, and a projected deficit of 145 million pesos by the end of the year.
24. Jorge Rojas Flores, *La dictadura de Ibáñez y los sindicatos 1927–1931* (Santiago: DIBAM, 1993), p. 170.
25. Speech at the University of Guadalajara, Mexico, 2 December 1972.
26. Lavretsky, p. 34.
27. José Bengoa, *Historia del Pueblo Mapuche* (Santiago: LOM, 2000), p. 398.
28. Arrate and Rojas v1, p. 155.

CHAPTER 3

1. Veneros, p. 138.
2. Salvador Allende, *Higiene mental y delincuencia* (Santiago: Chileamerica-CESOC, 1933), p. 8.

3. Ibid., p. 31–2.
4. James D. Cockcroft (ed.), *Salvador Allende Reader: Chile's Voice of Democracy* (New York: Ocean Press, 2000), p. 35.
5. Allende Senate Debates (ASD), Session 65a, 12 March 1968.
6. Jobet, pp. 79–80.
7. Interview in 'Chile Hoy', No. 43, April 1973.
8. Jobet, p. 90.
9. David F. Schmitz, *Thank God They're On Our Side: The United States and Right-Wing Dictatorships 1921–1965* (London: University of North Carolina Press, 1999), p. 47.
10. Orlando Millas, *La alborada democratica en Chile: Memorias* (Santiago: CESOC, 1993), p. 109.
11. Interview in 'Chile Hoy' magazine, No. 43, April 1973, published in Eduardo Gutierrez and Vladimir Sierpe (eds), *Salvador Allende. Entrevistas 1970–1973* (Santiago: Editare Editores Asociados, 2009), p. 182.
12. Carlos Briones in Francisco Flores (ed.), *Allende Cercano* (Zacatecas: UAZ, 1988), p. 164.
13. Thomas M. Klubock, 'Ranquil: Violence and Peasant Politics on Chile's Southern Frontier', in *A Century of Revolution*, eds Greg Grandin and Gilbert M. Joseph (London: Duke, 2010), p. 121.
14. Juan Gonzalo Rocha, 'Salvador Allende, un mason consecuente', in *Salvador Allende. Fragmentos para una historia*, ed. Fundacion Salvador Allende (Santiago: Fundacion Salvador Allende, 2008), p. 204.
15. Ibid., p. 199.
16. Ibid., p. 205.
17. Luis Alberto Sanchez, 'Siluetas latinoamericanas: Salvador Allende', *Nuevo Zig-Zag*, No. 2451, 15 March 1952, p. 17.
18. Veneros, p. 122.
19. ASD, Session 26a, Monday 26 July 1937.
20. Debray, p. 70.
21. Arturo Olavarria, a Radical Party member, quoted in Arrate and Rojas, vol. 1, p. 192–3.
22. Arrate and Rojas, vol. 1, p. 196.
23. Max Nolff, *Salvador Allende: El politico. El Estadista* (Santiago: Ediciones Documentas, 1993), p. 32.
24. Hortensia Bussi in Flores (ed.), p. 143–5.
25. Ibid., p. 122.
26. ASD, Session 31a, 30 July 1941.
27. Millas, *La alborada democratica en Chile*, p. 207.
28. Ibid., p. 287.
29. Speech to the Valparaiso Extraordinary Congress, 15 August 1943.
30. Speech in Homage to the Triumph of the Popular Front, October 1943.
31. Letter from the PS Central Committee to the Communist Party, 1 December 1943.
32. Arrate and Rojas, p. 106.

33. Before making the Communist Party illegal president Rios told his allies that he was coming under heavy international pressure to do so. Arrate and Rojas, p. 245.
34. Speech in the Caupolican Theatre, 1944.
35. Some of these even joined a paramilitary group known as ACHA (axe), or the Chilean Anti-Communist Alliance which also included far-right elements.
36. Nolff, p. 101. About US$6 billion today.
37. ASD, Sessions 14–15, 18 June 1948.

CHAPTER 4

1. Orlando Millas, *Memorias: la alborada democratica en Chile en tiempos del frente popular 1932–1947* (Santiago: CESOC, 1993), p. 206.
2. Sanchez, p. 17.
3. M. Labarca, p. 114.
4. Ibid., p. 87.
5. Osvaldo Puccio, *Un cuarto de siglo con Allende. Recuerdos de su secretario privado, Osvaldo Puccio* (Santiago: Editorial Emision, 1985), p. 24.
6. Volodia Teitelboim, *Un hombre de edad media*, 2nd edn (Santiago: Editorial Sudamericana, 2000), p. 343.
7. M. Labarca, p. 47.
8. Ozren Agnic, *Allende: El hombre y el politico. Memorias de un secretario privado* (Santiago: RIL editores, 2008), p. 28.
9. Carmen Lazo quoted in Veneros, p. 186.
10. E. Labarca, pp. 79–80.
11. M. Labarca, p. 54.
12. ASD, Session 19a, 16 January 1951.
13. ASD, Session 9a, 21 June 1951.
14. ASD, Session 19a, 16 January 1951.
15. ASD, Session 22a, 7 August 1951.
16. Chilean economists later estimated that in total these 'loans' had amounted to over US$800 million.
17. ASD, Session 4a, 2 June 1954.
18. Lavretsky, pp. 72–4.
19. Agnic, p. 44; Puccio, p. 68.
20. La Moneda is Chile's presidential palace in central Santiago.
21. Agnic, p. 45.
22. Puccio, p. 72; Arrate and Rojas, p. 330.
23. Jesus Manuel Martinez, *Salvador Allende* (Santiago: Catalonia, 2009), pp. 236–7.
24. Luis Corvalán,, 'Salvador Allende, Presidente del Pueblo', in *Salvador Allende: Presencia en la ausencia*, eds. Miguel Lawner, Hernan Soto and Jacobo Schatan (Santiago: LOM, 2008), p. 41.

25. Agnic, p. 46.
26. Jorquera, p. 32.
27. Despite campaigning as a leftist, Zamorano disappeared from politics until he was found supporting Pinochet's 'yes' campaign during the 1988 referendum. Agnic, p. 53.
28. In Chile, voters are registered to vote at particular numbered 'tables' within the polling station. Men and women vote at different tables. The votes are counted up and declared at each table, allowing a relatively accurate ongoing tally of votes.
29. This episode is recounted by Agnic, pp. 59–62, and M. Labarca, p. 67. Allende swore them to secrecy and it only came to light in 2008.

CHAPTER 5

1. Gaitan, p. 11.
2. Agnic, p. 71; ASD, Session 7a, 18 October 1967.
3. Debray, p. 73.
4. The daughter of the Colombian presidential candidate assassinated in 1948, Gaitan, p. 9.
5. ASD, Session 32a, 24 July 1960.
6. ASD, Session 24, 10 August 1960.
7. Agnic, p. 97.
8. The Chilean electoral system used the D'Hont method. Allende's vote was enough to get himself elected, but also contributed enough votes to the FRAP total to ensure the election of the communist candidate.
9. Castro Second Declaration of Havana, 4 February 1962.
10. Pablo Neruda, Confieso que he vivido, (Barcelona: Editorial Seix Barral, c. 1974), p. 155.
11. The 1975 Church Committee Report details CIA support for the PDC going back to the 1961 elections (Franck Church, John G. Tower et al. Covert Action in Chile 1963–1973, Staff Report of the Select Committee to Study Governmental Operations with respect to Intelligence Activities, United States Senate. December 18 1975).
12. This is the equivalent of nearly US$20 million today.
13. All these statistics are taken from the Church Committee Report 1975.
14. ASD, Session 52a, 6 May 1964.
15. Agnic, p. 140.
16. Puccio, p. 135; Agnic, p. 141.
17. Church Committee Report 1975, p. 15.
18. Jorquera, p. 59.
19. Cited in Martinez, p. 277.
20. The 'Chileanisation' of the copper industry was thought up by US executives at Kennecott, who needed investment in the El Teniente copper mine in order to increase production. Unwilling to take the money out of their

own profits, they envisioned a 'partnership' with Chilean investors. Since the Chilean private sector was too weak to take on this investment, they approached the government. See Nolff, pp. 210–12. US companies also pursued a similar policy in relation to nitrates.

21. *Discursos: Salvador Allende* (Havana: Editorial Ciencias Sociales, 1975), 'La Democracia Cristiana no es Revolucionaria', p. 12.

22. Ibid., p. 17.

23. E. Labarca, pp. 169–70.

24. Allende speech quoted in Nolff, pp. 38–46.

25. ASD, Session 7a, 18 October 1967.

26. Jorquera, p. 48.

27. During this period the CIA continued to 'support' right wing media, produce radio commentary shows and funded 'CIA-inspired editorials' in *El Mercurio*. Church Committee Report 1975, pp. 18–19.

28. M. Labarca, p. 120.

29. ASD, Session 65a, 12 March 1968.

30. ASD, Session 23a, 30 July 1969.

31. Luis Corvalán, *De lo vivido y lo peleado*, 2nd edn (Santiago: LOM Ediciones, 1999), p. 117.

32. M. Labarca, p. 162.

33. Luis Jerez, *Ilusiones y quebrantos (desde la memoria de un militante socialista)* (Santiago: Forja, 2007), p. 214.

34. Ibid., p. 215; Eduardo Gutierrez, *Ciudades en las sombras: Una historia no oficial del Partido Socialista de Chile* (Santiago: Editare, 2010), pp. 30–2.

35. Corvalán *De lo vivido y lo peleado*, p. 118.

36. Ibid., p. 117.

37. Some socialist testimonies assert that the Communists were pushing for their party to accept Baltra's candidacy, but this is hotly denied by the PC's then-leaders. See Joan Garcés, *Allende y la experiencia Chilena: las armas de la politica*, 3rd edn. (Santiago: Ediciones BAT, 1991), p. 241; Jerez, p. 217, Luis Corvalán, *El gobierno de Salvador Allende* (Santiago: LOM, 2003), p. 108; Millas *de O'Higgins a Allende* (Madrid: Ediciones Michay, 1980), p. 318.

38. Allende cited in Puccio, p. 135.

CHAPTER 6

1. Monica Gonzalez, *La Conjura: Los mil y un dias del golpe* (Santiago: Ediciones B, 2000), p. 54.

2. The Church Committee report states that 'labor [sic] and "community development" projects were deemed rather unsuccessful', and the precepts of Allende's campaign found 'almost universal support', Church Committee Report 1975, p. 19.

3. Equivalent to nearly US$6 million today.

4. Puccio, pp. 233–4.
5. 'Momio' – mummy, what the left called right-wing conservatives. Lisandro Otero, *Razon y fuerza de Chile: tres años de unidad popular* (Havana: Ciencias Sociales, 1980), p. 75.
6. *Discursos: Salvador Allende*, 'Discurso ante el pueblo de Santiago', 5 Septiembre 1970.
7. Peter Kornbluh, *The Pinochet File* (London: The New Press, 2003), p. 14.
8. Martinez, p. 318. Chilean presidential terms were limited to one six-year term.
9. Puccio, p. 272.
10. Gabriel Salazar, *Conversaciones con Carlos Altamirano. Memorias criticas* (Santiago: Random House, 2010), p. 263.
11. Valdes, p. 211. A secret CIA cable dated 5 September stated that 'If Tomic finishes third, this is tantamount to a rejection of all Frei and his government had sought to accomplish', see 'Concerns of President Frei' National Security Archive.
12. Kornbluh, p. 14, p. 17.
13. Ibid., p. 20.
14. Valdes, p. 207.
15. Max Marambio, *Las armas de ayer* (Santiago: Debate, 2007), p. 69; Enérico García Concha, *Todos los dias de la vida: Recuerdos de un militante del MIR chileno* (Santiago: Cuarto Propio, 2010), p. 67.
16. Valdes, p. 210.
17. Puccio, p. 272.
18. See 'NSC Meeting – Chile (NSSM 97)', 6 November 1970. National Security Archive.
19. NSC Memorandum 93, 'Policy Towards Chile', 9 November 1970. National Security Archive.
20. See NSC, Kissinger to President Nixon 'Covert Action Program – Chile', 25 November 1970. National Security Archive.
21. From the Programme of the Popular Unity.
22. The existence of two chambers and staggered elections contributed to enormous delays in passing legislation, sometimes of up to 20 years.
23. The latter was only reinstated in 1998.
24. Ironically land reform began under the auspices of the Alliance for Progress, and was envisioned as a way of preventing Marxist revolution.
25. Mireya Baltra, 'La participacion de los trabajadores en el gobierno popular del Presidente Salvador Allende', in *Salvador Allende: Presencia en la ausencia*, eds Miguel Lawner, Hernan Soto and Jacobo Schatan (Santiago LOM, 2008), p. 251.
26. First Message to Congress, 21 May 1971.
27. From the Programme of the Popular Unity.
28. Speech in the National Stadium, 5 November 1970.
29. See the work of Tomas Moulian for more on this.
30. Resolutions of the XXII PS Congress, La Serena, February 1971.

31. Valdes, p. 211.
32. The CIA provided significant funds to the PDC and the PN throughout Allende's government. See Kornbluh, p. 89. According to Garcés the money was actually given to the Frei faction of the PDC, strengthening its right wing.
33. Joan Garcés, *Allende y la experiencia Chilena: las armas de la política*, 3rd edn. (Santiago: Ediciones BAT, 1991), pp. 220–1.
34. First Message to Congress, 21 May 1971.
35. Garcés, pp. 211–12.
36. Speech on the Day of the Nationalisation of Copper, 11 July 1971.
37. Clodomiro Almeyda, *Reencuentro con mi vida* (Santiago: Las Ediciones del Ornitorrinco, 1987), pp. 172–9.
38. Gutierrez, p. 38.
39. Carlos Prats González, *Memorias: Testimonio de un soldado* (Santiago: Pehuén, 1985), p. 209.
40. Carlos Toro, *Memorias de Carlos Toro: La Guardia muere pero no se rinda...mierda*, La Vida es Hoy (Santiago: Partido Comunista de Chile, 2007), p. 352.
41. Corvalán, *El gobierno de Salvador Allende*, p. 191. According to Carlos Toro, the detective in charge of the investigation, a witness claimed that a Panamanian doctor exiled from Panama for organising an anti-Torrijos guerrilla group was the intellectual author of the killing. Since Panama was the home of Southcom, and several US military bases, suspicion remains that the CIA was somehow involved. It is also known that the CIA deployed 'false-flaggers' to Chile (see Kornbluh). However, the case was never solved. Toro, p. 353.
42. Garcés, p. 212.
43. Speech in the National Stadium on the First Anniversary of the Popular Government, 4 November 1971.
44. It did, but not until after the coup. In 1979 Altamirano split the PS, calling for its renovation which eventually led the PS to abandon Marxism and become a centre-left party that shared government with the PDC after the fall of Pinochet.
45. There are testimonies that provide evidence that the two had a somewhat competitive relationship. See Salazar, p. 234 and Felix Huerta, *El trabajo es vivir* (Santiago: Ediciones Ruben Dario, 2011), p. 118.
46. M. Labarca, p. 163.
47. Oscar Ibañez cited in Arrate and Rojas, vol. 2, p. 45.
48. Colonel Arellano Stark quoted in Gonzalez, p. 121.
49. Castro farewell speech, Santiago, 2 December 1971.
50. According to East German reports cited by Tanya Harmer, the Cubans had 'reservations and doubts' about the extent to which the UP's strategic goals could be achieved by democratic means alone, about Allende's tactics against the right, and they voiced concerns that the armed forces might

become the referees of the situation. Tanya Harmer, *Allende's Chile and the Inter-American Cold War* (University of North Carolina, 2011), p. 152.

51. Joan Garcés, Allende's former political adviser, recalled this incident at an event called '25 years after the military coup', held in Santiago in September 1998. It can be found here: http://www.diarioreddigital.cl/index.php?option=com_content&view=article&id=10237:allende-la-democracia-cristiana-y-las-verdades-de-una-historia-silenciada-&catid=128:debate&Itemid=102, accessed December 2012.

52. See Kornbluh, p. 90.

53. Eden Medina, 'Designing Freedom, Regulating a Nation: Socialist Cybernetics in Allende's Chile', *Journal of Latin American Studies*, No. 38, 2006.

54. Franck Gaudichaud, 'Construyendo "Poder Popular": El movimiento sindical, la CUT y las luchas obreras en el periodo de la Unidad Popular', in Julio Pinto Vallejos, *Cuando hicimos historia: La experiencia de la Unidad Popular* (Santiago: LOM, 2005), p. 99.

55. Harmer, pp. 193, 157–8.

56. Valdes, p. 239.

CHAPTER 7

1. Alain Joxe, *Las fuerzas armadas en el sistema politico de chile* (Santiago: Editorial Universitaria, 1970), p. 42–3.

2. Verónica Valdivia Ortiz de Zárate, *El golpe despues del golpe: Leigh vs Pinochet Chile 1960–1980* (Santiago: LOM, 2003), p. 35.

3. Felipe Agüero, 'A Political Army in Chile: Historical Assessment and Prospects for the New Democracy', in *Political Armies*, eds Kees Koonings and Dirk Kruijt (London: Zed, 2002), p. 117.

4. Pickering quoted in Gonzalez, p. 32.

5. Admiral Merino quoted in Gonzalez, pp. 38–9. Merino was one of the coup plotters.

6. Report quoted in Gonzalez, pp. 26–7.

7. Second Message to Congress, 21 May 1972.

8. Allende quoted in Verónica Valdivia Ortiz de Zárate, 'Salvador Allende y las fuerzas armadas en la transicion al socialismo', in *Salvador Allende: Fragmentos para una historia*, ed. Fundacion Salvador Allende (Santiago: Fundacion Salvador Allende, 2008), p. 115.

9. On the day of the coup the MIR had 50 armed and trained men ready for action, with another 400 trained but unarmed, and the PS 100, with a few more in Allende's security team. Patricio Z. Quiroga, *El GAP: La escolta de Allende* (Santiago: Aguilar, 2001), pp. 150–2. The Communists later admitted to 1,000 members trained in the use of automatic weapons, but these were unarmed and dispersed across the country. The Chilean armed forces in 1973 consisted of over 60,000 men.

10. Valdivia, '*El golpe despues del golpe*', p. 79.
11. General Mario Sepulveda quoted in Gonzalez, p. 246.
12. Prats, p. 471.
13. Prats, p. 452.
14. Prats, p. 485.
15. Quoted in Gonzalez, p. 326.
16. Alfredo Joignant, the Director of the civilian investigations police, quoted in Gonzalez, p. 210.
17. La Nacion, 20 April 2008, 'Guillermo Claverie – yo no mate al comandante Araya'. Suspicions remain that members of Naval Intelligence took part in the killing since they had been cooperating with Fatherland and Liberty for some time.
18. Salazar, p. 290.
19. Gaitan, p. 118.
20. Speech to the CUT 25 July 1973.
21. Prats, pp. 478–80.
22. Altamirano recalls Prats telling him 'I have an enormous appreciation for the President, but this is not *my* revolution.' in Salazar, p. 242.
23. Kornbluh, p. 111.
24. Kornbluh, p. 95.
25. According to Jaime Gazmuri, then president of the MAPU, at a meeting with the CUT, Allende and Prats, Pinochet proposed to develop a defence plan based on combining military units with workers. Interview in *El Mercurio*, 12 October 2003.
26. Garcés, p. 385.
27. Prats, p. 485.
28. Gutierrez, p. 20.
29. Payita quoted in E. Labarca, p. 352.
30. Jorquera, p. 88.
31. Patricio Guijon quoted in E. Labarca, p. 354.
32. Testimony of these final moments is confused. This account is based on the various testimonies collected by E. Labarca, pp. 409–12.

CHAPTER 8

1. See Garcés, Joan '25 Years After the Coup' September 1998.
2. Several members of Chile's current right-wing government were present at this ceremony.

CHAPTER 9

1. Interview in 'Clarin' 13 September 1970.
2. Debray, p. 69.

3. Jorge Arrate, *Salvador Allende, ¿sueño o proyecto?* (Santiago: LOM, 2008), p. 42.

4. Corvalán, *El gobierno de Salvador Allende*, p. 264.

5. Luis Bonilla-Molina and Haiman El Troudi, *Historia de la revolucion Bolivariana* (Caracas: Ministerio de Cultura, 2004), p. 52.

Index

Printed and bound by CPI Group (UK) Ltd, Croydon, CR0 4YY

03/09/2023

08108280-0001